TIME
WELL
SPENT

70001345176 X

TIME WELL SPENT

Getting things done through effective time management

Lyndon Jones and Paul Loftus

KOGAN PAGE

London and Philadelphia

First published in Great Britain and the United States in 2009 by Kogan Page Limited

120 Pentonville Road
London N1 9JN
United Kingdom
www.koganpage.com

525 South 4th Street, #241
Philadelphia PA 19147
USA

© Paul Loftus and Lyndon Jones, 2009

The right of Paul Loftus and Lyndon Jones to be identified as the authors of this work has been asserted by them in accordance with the Copyright, Designs and Patents Act 1988.

ISBN 978 0 7494 5649 8

British Library Cataloguing-in-Publication Data

A CIP record for this book is available from the British Library.

Library of Congress Cataloging-in-Publication Data

Jones, Lyndon H. (Lyndon Hamer)
    Time well spent : getting things done through effective time management / Lyndon Jones and Paul Loftus.
        p. cm.
    Includes bibliographical references and index.
    ISBN 978-0-7494-5649-8
  1. Time management. 2. Self-management (Psychology) I. Loftus, Paul. II. Title.
    HD69.T54J665 2009
    650.1'1—dc22

                                                    2009008503

Typeset by JS Typesetting Ltd, Porthcawl, Mid Glamorgan
Printed and bound in India by Replika Press Pvt Ltd

Contents

Figures

Tables

About the authors

Following service in HM Forces, Lyndon Jones studied at Manchester University and undertook postgraduate studies at the Manchester College of Science and Technology. He worked in industry as a line manager before taking a teacher's certificate. For six years he was head of a department of management and business studies. From 1965 until 1990 he was Principal of the South West London College (the equivalent of an American Business School).

He has served on many councils, committees and boards, including:

Business Education Council (to which he was nominated by the Secretary of State for Education);
Council for Accreditation of Correspondence Colleges (again being nominated by the Secretary of State for Education);
National Examination Board in Supervisory Management (vice-chairman);
BBC Further Education Advisory Committee;
British Accreditation Council for Independent Further and Higher Education;
British Rail Joint Industrial Training Board;
Committees of the Engineering Industry Training Board, Construction Industry Training Board and Shipbuilding Training Board;
International Federation of Training and Development Organizations (IFTDO);
Board of Indian journal, *Drishti*;
Court of Governors of the International University of Management in Namibia;
Council of ARTDO International;
Employers with a Heart Advisory Board (Singapore) (Honorary co-chairman and advisor);
Editorial board, Indian Journal of Education and Training.

He founded and for 21 years was chairman of the Association of Business Executives, of which he is currently CEO. He is chairman of the Association of Business and Administrative Computing, and founded the Association of Business Practitioners. He was editorial director of the monthly publication *Education and Training* for 22 years and for some years was editor of the *Free Trader*.

He is the author of a number of books and pamphlets and has had articles published in the UK and overseas journals and newspapers. He worked with the Council of Europe and produced a report on the regulation of private higher education. He has extensive experience as a consultant, trainer and team leader, having worked in western Europe, south-east Asia, the United States and Africa. For a number of years he was a consultant with the Hong Kong Productivity Council. He was awarded the Management and HRD Excellence Award from ARTDO in recognition of services to education.

Paul Loftus is a Montreal-based international management development consultant, an industrial psychologist and freelance journalist. He leads seminars in several areas related to dealing effectively with others, oneself and one's organization. He has conducted seminars across Canada and in the United States, Bermuda, the UK, Ireland, France, Belgium, the Netherlands, Germany, Austria, Iceland, Turkey, Qatar, Kuwait, United Arab Emirates, Saudi Arabia, Egypt, Sudan, Malaysia, Singapore, Indonesia, China, Hong Kong and Australia.

Over the last few years he has earned an excellent reputation for his work in performance management, time and productivity management, assertiveness training, stress management, selection and retention techniques, business writing, effective presentation skills, media interviewing, managing diversity, conflict resolution, effective negotiation skills, professional development for executive secretaries and administrative/personal assistants, dynamics of management; many skills-oriented areas including communication, situational leadership, feedback, analysing performance problems, motivation and conducting effective meetings.

As an industrial psychologist he has appeared on CBC TV's current affairs programme 'Take 30', CFCF TV's talk show 'Montreal AM Live', ZBM Television in Bermuda and CBC's radio programme 'Home Run'. He has been interviewed by Canada's *Globe and Mail*, *Montreal Gazette*, *Montreal Downtowner*, *Verve* magazine and *Chatelaine*, as well as the UK's *Sunday Telegraph* and *Executive PA* magazine, Bermuda's *Royal Gazette* and *Mid-Ocean News*, Malaysia's *Berita Harian* and *Star*, and Indonesia's *Bisnis Indonesia*. He has also appeared on CBC's talk show 'Geraldine', and for 25 years co-hosted a community television programme in Montreal. He has published many articles and is a well-known speaker with engagements in Canada, the United States, the UK, Germany, the United Arab Emirates, Argentina, Taiwan, Singapore, Indonesia, Malaysia, India and Ireland.

He graduated from University College Dublin with a BComm, and from Concordia University in Montreal with a BA in psychology. He holds an MSc in industrial and organizational psychology from Lamar University, Texas. He is a Fellow of the Institute of Canadian Bankers and was awarded Associate Insurance Broker membership of the Insurance Brokers' Association of the Province of Quebec. He holds a certificate in journalism from Concordia University, where he is currently also completing a certificate in public relations. He is a licensed industrial psychologist in Quebec.

He is president of the Ireland–Canada Chamber of Commerce. He is also the co-founder and a director of the Montreal Trainers' Group. His other professional affiliations include membership of the Quebec Association for Adult Learning, the Canadian Society for Training and Development, the American Society for Training and Development, the American Management Association, the Irish Institute of Training and Development, the Asian Regional Training and Development Organization, the Montreal Press Club, and others.

Preface

This book is the result of a deep interest by both authors in its topic. It is based on the premise that it is important to know yourself before you start to manage how you deal with time. You cannot really manage time because it is a constant, and you cannot do anything to increase or decrease the number of hours in a day. All you can do is manage yourself in relation to the amount of time you have at your disposal. Time is the great equalizer: we all have 24 hours a day, no matter how much money we have and regardless of our race, religion, creed, colour, age and position or status in society.

The book is divided into two sections. The first six chapters deal with personal choice, while the ensuing 13 deal with generic skills for managing your time more effectively. The book starts with life goals in the first chapter and the next two chapters deal with helping you to attain them. Chapter 4 helps you to get to know yourself better; this will help you see how you as an individual deal with time. Chapter 5 deals with the problem of procrastination; those of us who are chronic procrastinators will find some helpful ideas here. Chapter 6 deals with the area of mental set and perception and their effect on time management.

The skills with which the book deals are those we did not learn in school, college or university. Yet they are skills that are essential for success in business. They include such topics as analysing your time and using it to best effect, organization (workload and workplace), handling interruptions, managing information and technology, delegation, conducting meetings effectively, and the often-overlooked skills needed to deal with a boss who wastes your time. Today all these skills are as basic as reading, writing and listening. In this book you will find them all clearly and helpfully described. Read about them, study them, practise them – and soon you will be taking control of your life and your time.

Introduction

If you can fill the unforgiving minute
With sixty seconds' worth of distance run,
Yours is the earth and everything that's in it…

Rudyard Kipling, 'If'

Numerous books and articles have been published on time management. So you might ask, 'Why another book on the subject?' At the same time, many time-management programmes have been run. But the return on investment from a high percentage of these has been quite low. Two factors in particular have contributed to this:

- They assumed that participants had control of their own roles. Yet most people's time is governed by other people's demands – and superiors' priorities can change with head-spinning speed.
- Many workshops were designed around a package rather than the specific needs of the participants. They focused on the 'how to'. But what works with one type of personality may not work with another. For example, a person's inefficient use of time may stem from time wasting – such as procrastination or the ineffective handling of information – or from failure to distinguish between efficiency and effectiveness.

Effective time management does not result from the application of an inflexible set of principles or techniques. People are different. Understanding yourself is essential for effective time management. To be able to plan your future, you have to be able to anticipate your behaviour in future situations. This requires self-knowledge.

Many of us know our particular time bandits but to change one's time-management behaviour one has to want to do so.

Perfectionists have to learn to do things only to the standard required. Providing people with time-saving devices and sending them on programmes is not usually sufficient to get them to unlearn old habits, and develop and practise new behaviour patterns.

Because of changes in the global economy, the need to discard old habits and adopt new and more efficient ones has never been greater. Among these changes are:

- Globalization necessitates a greater understanding of the cultural differences in attitudes towards time. In many Eastern cultures time is seen as polychronic: endless, without beginning or end. Time limits are not part of the vocabulary. This is in marked contrast with those who embrace the western concept of time, in which it is seen as monochronic or linear, a valuable commodity because of its scarcity. In this view, time is compartmentalized, organized and controlled.
- Technology, particularly computers, is having a tremendous impact, not least by enabling a growing number of people to work from home or remote from their employing organization. This requires different disciplines.

De-layering and re-engineering have wiped out tranches of management. Organizations have fewer people, which means that the survivors must work harder or more effectively.

With old organization structures being wiped out, many jobs are less defined than 20 years ago and new methods of working are required. Witness the increase in team working. Sometimes there is rotating leadership, or teams are leaderless. In these situations it is more difficult for the individual to prioritize their tasks. In many cases a team is required only for the execution of a single task or project; it then disbands and the individual becomes part of another team. Learning to be an effective team manager, or participant, makes more demands on a person's effective time management.

The virtual corporation, the virtual office, outsourcing, multi-skilled teams and the like are changing people's lives. The job is not dead but unconditional lifetime employment is. In turn, a new concept is developing. Employers now have an obligation to provide opportunity for self-improvement to ensure lifelong employability. And employees have to take charge of their own careers. So clarity of objectives is vital. In the same way as we budget our finances, we also must budget our time.

The four ages

Shakespeare wrote about the seven ages of man. Today for many of us there are four ages:

Preparing for work. This period has lengthened markedly in the past few years, as evidenced by the growth in higher education.

Working. Fewer years are now spent working (although in view of the greying of the population in some countries, this trend has been reversed). Meanwhile there is a greater focus on getting a more balanced work–life relationship. Many people are cash-rich, time-poor (CRTP). Witness the situation in the USA, where a high percentage of people only have two weeks' annual holiday. Hence the trend towards GAPI (get a person in) rather than DIY (do it yourself).

The third age. This can be the period over which a person has greatest control of their life.

Decline. Dependency and Death.

The third age is a relatively new phenomenon. An increasing number of people are leaving the workforce at a much earlier age, concurrent with an increasing lifespan. Simultaneously, the quality of life is being enhanced. Disability among the elderly is declining sharply, with bone and organ transplants, corneal laser surgery and other modern medical 'miracles'.

For many, the third age can be the golden years. People are healthy and, with proper planning, have a reasonable income yet without the major financial commitments of previous years, such as paying for children's education or buying a home. Importantly, they also have greater control of their own lives. However senior they might have been during their working years, perhaps as CEO or head of an organization, they would have been answerable to someone, such as a board of directors or a governing body. But in the third age, within reason, people can do what they want when they want.

So the aim of the authors of this book is to assist you to:

- focus on your objectives, thereby enriching your life at every stage;
- analyse your strengths and take corrective action in the case of any weaknesses, such as procrastination;
- use your time more effectively.

Then the rest is up to you.

After all, it stands to reason when you have learnt to manage your time more effectively, you will be less stressed and in greater control of your life.

01

Determining and attaining your life goals

> Always aim high. If you aim at the stars, you certainly should not end up with a handful of mud. If you aim at nothing in life, you are liable to hit nothing. If you don't know where you are going, it doesn't really matter which route you take. Successful people always have one thing in common: they all know where they are going. Each has a goal. Anything the mind can conceive and believe, it can achieve.
>
> William James

Traditional education was designed to teach people to be obedient, well behaved and diligent, and to accept their status in life. It was assumed that our position and standing were inevitably determined by forces beyond our control. The few who disputed this idea were often regarded as unstable and potential troublemakers.

In a growing number of countries these attitudes are no longer in keeping with the fast-changing world around us. Many of the old authoritarian hierarchies have collapsed and others will do so. Whether they were states such as the USSR or corporations such as General Motors, none has been immune to the revolutionary changes. The twin forces of technology and economics have destroyed the hierarchical constraints.

New structures have emerged which are much flatter, more flexible and in which employees have a very different relationship with the organization. In these new relationships there is little scope for the old notions of loyalty and advancement. Individuals are responsible for their own careers and destinies.

Despite what many of us have been brought up to believe and the changes that are occurring in the world, all of us can have greater command over our own destinies *if we really want to*. This requires us not only to be single-minded and assertive but also to exercise an appropriate degree of self-control. In this way we can achieve our desired ends without harming the other people who share a similar way of life.

By the time you have read this chapter, we hope you will have absorbed *and acted upon* some ideas for determining your goals, your priorities and your methods of achieving them. It is important to remember that goal setting is hard work and requires time and effort.

Personal SWOT analysis

A powerful tool to use in connection with the attainment of your life goals is the completion of a personal SWOT analysis – strengths, weaknesses, opportunities and threats. This valuable tool can be used to enable you to list all your actual and perceived strengths and weaknesses in respect of skills, attitudes, likes and dislikes.

As you cannot build performance on weakness, ask yourself, 'What are my strengths?' Most people think they know what they are good at but often they are wrong. To find out your strengths, use feedback analysis, ie when you make a key decision, write down what you expect will result. Six or nine months later compare results to expectations. When this is repeated over a year or two your real strengths become clear.

Once you know what your strengths are, concentrate on them, and work on improving them – in particular your areas of high competence.

Feedback analysis also reveals that a major reason for poor performance is not knowing enough or disregarding the importance of knowledge outside one's own speciality.

On completion of the SWOT analysis and feedback analysis, you can prepare a personal action plan to facilitate the attainment of your goals. In doing so, recognize that you will probably need help from others to achieve your plan.

TOWS analysis offers a slight variation to the more traditional SWOT analysis. It uses the same principles but focuses on the negative external factors first in order to turn them into positive factors or 'opportunities'. This idea of looking at the situation from a different perspective has been highlighted by Heinz Weihrich, Professor of Management at the University of San Francisco. He points out that 'weakness is an absence of strength, and corporate development to overcome an existing weakness may become a distinct strategy for the company'.

Goal setting: what do you want to achieve?

People are often very vague about answering this question. They may give such answers as:

- realizing my potential;
- having the satisfaction of doing my job well;
- ensuring financial security.

Such fuzzy ideas, though admirable as general aims, are too imprecise to stand much chance of being fully realized.

Make a list of all the things you want to do, to try, to achieve, to experience, to possess before the end of your life. You may also ask yourself questions such as:

- What makes me feel fully alive?
- What do I do well?
- What do I need to learn to do given my aspirations?
- How do I turn wishes into plans?
- What do I start doing now?
- What should I stop doing now?

You should distinguish between short-term and long-term goals.

Where appropriate, it can be helpful to visualize your goals in the greatest possible detail.

Once a goal has been achieved, reward yourself.

Some examples of goal setting would be along the following lines:

I intend to reach board level in my company before I am 40.

I aim to get married between the ages of 30 and 35 and have two children.

Within the next ten years I intend to leave salaried employment and be running my own seaside restaurant.

Before I retire, my partner and I intend to visit all the continents and at least 25 different countries.

I intend to be selected to represent my country in the next Olympic Games.

See if you can identify for yourself five major life goals, things you want to achieve. There are a number of useful techniques for helping you in this.

Some useful techniques for life goal setting

Goal setting is a major factor in personal and management success. In setting goals you may be seeking security, enjoyment or self-fulfilment. One approach is to use Maslow's hierarchy of needs. He suggested that individuals were motivated by five levels of need, namely:

Physiological. These include food, shelter, clothing, heat and light. Each of these basic needs can be satisfied by income from employment.

Security. Once the physiological needs have been met, an individual will seek security both at home and at work in respect of tenure and living standards.

Social. Most people want to feel wanted and belong to a community. This is the case both when at work and in non-working time.

Esteem. People need recognition. This can take the form of personal possessions or self-respect.

Self-actualization. Maslow saw this as the highest level of need concerning creative activity and the search for personal fulfilment.

Another useful tool to help you arrive at life goals is to make an analysis of the time you spend on various aspects of your life. Then ask the questions set out in Table 1.1.

With the aid of the prompting you get from the answers to these questions, it should be possible to arrive at some fresh aims in life to reduce some of the pressures and discomfort which currently rob you of the time you would prefer to be spending on more satisfying activities.

One technique to help you sharpen up on the planning of your long-range goals is to define a perfect day. It should not be a fantasy day but a real day – one fully satisfying in terms of work, relationship with family and friends, and physical environment.

Table 1.1 Work and personal time

Some questions to ask yourself	Mostly	Sometimes	Seldom
Am I spending my time in the way I really want to?			
Do I find myself doing things I don't want to do?			
Do I enjoy work?			
Do I work long hours?			
Do I take work home in the evenings?			
Do I take work home at weekends?			
Do I feel tense in my job?			
Do I feel insecure in my job?			
Do I enjoy family life?			

Do I spend as much time as I would like:
  with my family?
  keeping fit?
  keeping up to date professionally?
  pursuing my hobbies?			

Do I feel guilty when I'm not being active?			
Do I have enough discretionary time?			

The time when you set or review your goals is important. For many, a good time coincides with a major festive season. This is often a time when New Year resolutions are in your mind; at the same time there is a lull in work. It is a good time to be reflective – what did I accomplish during the past year and how did that mesh in with my goals; what do I want to accomplish in the next year?

Your personal action plan

In order to make progress towards achieving your lifetime goals, it is necessary to define some shorter-term targets to provide intermediate mileposts along the way. To arrive at these, try working backwards from a point, say, five or ten years from now, at which you will have fully achieved each of your longer-term goals, and see what intermediate steps will be necessary in each year (with shorter intervals during the first year). With your goals and these targets clearly fixed in your mind, you can more readily notice essential opportunities during the intervening period. Here are some examples of intermediate targets:

> Within the next three years I intend to learn sufficient Spanish to be able to converse freely with the locals at my regular holiday resort in Spain/Mexico/Argentina.
> If I have not succeeded in obtaining a promotion in my present job to my boss's level within the next 18 months, I will then seek an equivalent job elsewhere.
> By the time I am 30, I will possess a four-bedroom house in the country within commuting distance of London, Dublin, New York, Singapore, Sydney, Cape Town, Montreal, Kuala Lumpur (or wherever you intend to work).

Note that these are all specific intentions with a definite timescale attached. It is important that they should be realistic in terms of the resources you are likely to have available, because only then can they form the basis of your personal action plan.

This requires you to define a set of specific steps you intend to take to achieve these targets. They should consist of a sequence of timed steps, starting with the very first action you intend to take tomorrow, next week or at the beginning of next month in order to get things going. Thereafter, the sequence should show, in date order, the other steps you need to take within the next review period (three or six months might be suitable for this) in order to ensure that you are remaining on target for achieving your life goals. Table 1.2 shows an example.

Now it's your turn again. Don't delay. Try it on your own situation, and stick to it! You will need a separate action plan for each of the current targets of your life goal areas. In short: get ready, get set, and GO for self-development, for problem solving and for life enrichment.

Table 1.2 Personal action plan for the next six months

Life goal: retiring to Spain
Short-term target: fluent in Spanish within three years

Step	Timing	Action
1	Tonight	Share this plan with my partner
2	Next Friday	Enrol for Spanish lessons next term/semester at my local college
3	Next pay day	Purchase CDs of conversational Spanish
4	All next month	Get away from television for an hour from 9–10 pm two evenings a week to practise with the CDs
5	Three months hence	Book our next holiday in Spain

Periodic review

Things will rarely go exactly to plan. Goals should be flexible. Goals can change. Goals and action plans should be reviewed at regular intervals to ensure that they are still relevant and realistic. They must constantly be checked for incompatibility with one another, or inconsistency with your chosen current or changing lifestyle. The attainment of one particular goal, eg studying for a doctorate, may not be consistent with another goal, eg spending more time with your children while they are still young. Priorities should be re-examined periodically to ensure that you are spending your precious time on working towards those ends that are going to provide the greatest long-term satisfaction. The personal reality check below is a useful guide to some of the questions you should be asking yourself during these reviews.

Personal reality check

To check that your current goals are still realistic, ask yourself periodically: 'Am I accomplishing the goals that are really important to me?' In turn, this may require answering further questions such as:

Personal life:
- – Do my career goals equate with my life goals?
- – Is my life as I would wish it to be?

Career:
- – Am I at the level I should have reached by now?
- – If not, why not?
- – What, if anything, must I or could I do about it?

Work:
- – Do I honestly enjoy my job?
- – Am I seeking self-fulfilment outside my work commitments?
- – Am I getting to where I want to be?

Salary:
- – Am I being fairly remunerated for my contribution to my employer?

- Is my total remuneration package at the anticipated level?
- Has my salary growth rate been consistent?

Having made the reality check, you will be in a better position to decide what you are really willing to work for, as opposed to mere wishful thinking. When you have determined what this is, assess what needs to be done to achieve it, then apply the best method you can devise for doing so.

Some people avoid goal setting through fear of failure. Their reason is that if they don't set goals, they can't fail. There can also be fear of success. Some people don't value themselves enough to feel they deserve it.

Another technique you may find helpful for checking the effectiveness of your target setting is the SPIRO method, reproduced here by courtesy of 3M (UK) Ltd.

SPIRO: criteria for effective target setting

When setting long-term goals or short-term targets, good intentions are not enough – the results need to be specified and observable.

The first criterion is *Specificity*. Generalized objectives are less useful than specific targets that imply next steps or behaviours that need to be changed. Examples:

Non-specific: to learn a foreign language.
Specific: next September, to enrol for an evening course in beginner's French; to attend at least two-thirds of the classes; to undertake at least three hours of private study per week.
Non-specific: to improve my sales record next year.
Specific: to achieve five per cent more sales next year.

The second criterion is *Performance*. Performance-oriented target statements are more effective than non-performance statements in guiding what a person is going to do. Examples:

Non-performance: to qualify in French.

Performance: to take and pass with credit a beginner's French conversation course before next June.

Non-performance: to gain the respect of my departmental colleagues.

Performance: to make at least one constructive point at each departmental meeting.

The third criterion is *Involvement*. This is the extent to which the job holder is personally involved in the target. Example:

Non-involvement: to have my manager treat me better.

Involvement: to reinforce my manager whenever given constructive feedback.

The fourth criterion is *Realism*. This is whether the target is readily attainable within the abilities and resources of the job holder. Example:

Non-realistic: to be promoted to an executive position by the end of the year.

Realistic: to take a course in management skills next quarter.

The final criterion is *Observability*. This has to do with whether other people can see the result, ie whether it is obvious or not that the job holder has met the criterion. Example:

Non-observable: to feel confident.

Observable: to reduce the frequency with which I preface my opinions with 'Well, I don't really know for sure, but…'

If you can apply these five criteria to your own life goals, short-term targets or work objectives, the result will be a much better understanding of exactly where you are going and what actions you intend to take to get there.

Finally, it is often useful to be able to let yourself off the hook when you are deliberating about possible alternative courses of action facing you in your life or your career. A technique for this is the balance-sheet grid (developed by Irving Janis and Leon Mann), which requires you to answer questions about potential risks and gains for each alternative action, classified into the following four categories:

- tangible gains or losses for yourself;
- tangible gains or losses for significant people involved in or affected by your decision;
- your own feelings of self-approval or disapproval;
- the approval or disapproval of significant people involved or affected.

You set out each alternative on a balance-sheet grid, which describes your positive arguments ('gains') and negative arguments ('losses') in each of these four categories. The example in Table 1.3 relates to a decision about early retirement.

With the full range of significant factors displayed before you (and available for sharing with your spouse or significant other, if appropriate) you are less likely to force yourself into taking a hasty decision based on inadequate data, and which you may later regret.

Midlife

For many of us, midlife has fewer restrictions than our earlier years. This is a time when you have gained confidence through experience. The absence of family commitments leaves you free for personal development, job opportunities, retraining and exploration that may have previously been hindered by lack of finance and family ties.

To retain vigour, you must have a future, with goals, ambitions and interests to be fulfilled. Having spent a great deal of your life working towards security, you may make the mistake of selling your soul for security, and sacrifice variety. Then stagnation sets in. There is still an attitude that it is not natural to develop in

Table 1.3 Balance-sheet grid for early retirement

	Gains	Losses
Tangible gains or losses for self	More freedom of choice Opportunities to pursue different income-earning activities End of day-to-day work pressures More time for golf Expect to live longer	Substantial reduction of income Loss of company car Loss of expense account Loss of some valuable social and working contacts End of P.A.
Tangible gains or losses for others	Less irritable when at home More time to spend with family	Drop in family standard of living Loss of status
Self-approval or disapproval	Foolish to continue to suffer stress from boss	Will no longer use full skills and abilities Will feel loss of self-esteem
Approval or disapproval of significant others	Family will be pleased to see more of me Organizers of local charities will be glad of more support from me Community organizations will be pleased	Colleagues and juniors will miss me Friends may feel I have become a less interesting person, or even a bore

middle age, whereas in fact this is when you have most time to do so, with fewer other people to consider first. We have been taught that the years of infancy and adolescence are the formative ones, but there is no reason why this process of development should ever cease. The midlife renaissance is when a person is able to shake off the stereotype and ignore the calendar.

Today neither men nor women expect to stay in one job for life, or even in one career. There are many reassessment periods, bringing a newly awakened capacity and greater depth. Time without ties is a precious rarity, but without shape or structure or value it is not worth as much. You need to retain a sense of purpose and identity.

The third age

Many people spend more time planning a holiday than planning for retirement. This can result in problems following retirement, for much of our identity and sense of purpose are tied up in work. Further, work can be your main creative outlet. So analyse your strengths, how you use them at work and how you will use them in retirement.

Invest time to ensure you find fulfilment. This may require you to dig deeply into yourself. Then develop an action plan with your partner. All this should be done well before the retirement date looms.

Many organizations offer programmes to prepare their employees for retirement, so if you are offered the opportunity to take one, do so. Alternatively, online programmes and specialist counsellors are available.

The possibility spectrum

As a practical guide for effective handling of the future, think towards a reasonable time period ahead, eg six months or a year. Then answer the following questions:

What is the worst outcome that could happen to me during this period?
What is the best outcome that could happen to me during this period?
What is the most likely outcome that could happen to me during this period?

A further description of each of these outcomes or events can often be assisted by means of a simple checklist including such

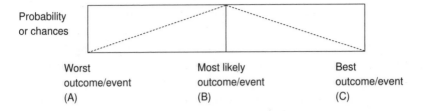

Figure 1.1 Probability distribution

factors as status, role, responsibilities, influence, and any others considered relevant. When the answers to these questions become available, there will be the beginning of a probability distribution, shown in Figure 1.1.

By defining these three events all the possibilities will have been covered – at least as far as your own imaginings are concerned. Further, according to normal probability distribution (the dotted line in Figure 1.1), the greater chances lie near the centre; and those chances are progressively reduced towards the extremes of the distribution.

It is always useful to have in mind what might transpire if the worst or best happens, however small the likelihood. Again, it is useful to write down the answers to these questions:

How would you feel if event A happened?
How would you feel if events B and C happened?

Concluding comments

With effective planning, the opportunity to achieve your life goal has never been greater. Until recently the manner in which executives balanced their professional and private lives was not considered by employers as something that was relevant. What executives did outside their work was not considered anything to do with the employer. Today, that view is changing as the dividing line between private and working life becomes blurred.

A number of factors have contributed to this. First, computer technology enables work which would once have been completed only in the office to be done at home or while travelling. Second, there are more dual-career families. Multinational companies in particular are acutely aware that the domestic arrangements of an employee can be as vital to the success of a career move as that of a foreign assignment.

And third, de-layering, re-engineering and the like have reduced career opportunities. Those who are disappointed that they have gone as high as they are likely to get in their professional life may compensate by expanding their out-of-work activities, many of which can begin to resemble alternative jobs.

Now, having determined your life goals and methods for attaining them, how will you use your time?

02

Increasing your leisure time

Time is such a funny thing, of logic it's bereft,
Because the more of it you have, the less you will have left.

Richard Bradshaw

Time is a unique resource: you cannot buy it, beg it, borrow it, rent it, store it, steal it or stretch it; it is perishable and irreplaceable. The past is irretrievable, the future is only a concept; today is all we have to work with.

From the humblest and poorest among us to the grandest and wealthiest, we all have the same allowance of only 24 hours in each day and 168 hours in each week. These boundaries exist no matter how we choose to spend our time. If we are to get the best from time, we must manage it more thoughtfully and effectively.

Managing time is becoming increasingly complicated. For many of us, balancing responsibilities at work and home and at the same time finding time to enjoy our private lives proves increasingly challenging. For example, for many employees time is the new money. Certainly many feel they have less time. This is because of the proliferation of choices and activities open to us these days. People have so much more they want to do now than they did in the past, hence work gets in the way.

Because it is such a precious commodity, we need to be selective about giving our time to others. Thus the choice of how much time, if any, we are prepared to give to every other person in our lives is an important indicator of how we feel about them. We tend to devote more of our time to the people we like and less to those whose company we find painful. One of the unkindest things we can say about another person is that they are a 'waste of time'. So by giving time to a person, or offering to do so, we are tacitly indicating that they are important to us. In private life this means that we care about them; at work it means that we accord them high status or esteem.

Hence, time management should not be narrowly defined. On the contrary, it is something that plays a very important role in contributing to the richness of our life.

An inch of gold will not buy an inch of time.

Chinese proverb

Our attitude to punctuality extends this concept. Are we more punctual with some people than with others? Do we drift in late to meetings called by senior managers, or only to those convened by our peers or team members? How much respect, or lack of it, does this show? If we are late for meetings with a senior manager, we run the risk of a reprimand; but if the most senior manager turns up late, the others present will usually accept the delay for a while, even if no explanation is forthcoming. Indeed, some delays are deliberate. They are intended to indicate superior status, as is the case in Japan.

Time speaks, and when it comes to punctuality it speaks very loudly. Can you imagine someone arriving late for a job interview, a flight, a train, a court appearance, or a meeting with a member of parliament?

Valuing your own time

How much do you value your time? If you are on a fixed salary at work, with an agreed working week, any loss of time is relatively easy to calculate. Table 2.1 provides a ready reckoner for calculating the cost of those lost moments and is a salutary reminder of how much is involved when several people are waiting around simultaneously (eg at meetings) for another person to arrive. If you are self-employed, with a fixed hourly or daily rate that you could use otherwise by charging out, perhaps you are more conscious than most of the cost of any delay because it can directly affect your income. For most people, however, loss of time is at worst regarded as a passing annoyance and more often is shrugged off with a casual disregard or not even noticed

Table 2.1 What is your time worth in financial terms?

Annual salary	*Calculations apply in any given unit of currency*					
	Cost of each unit of your time					
	1 min	*5 mins*	*10 mins*	*30 mins*	*1 hour*	*1 working day*
10,000	0.05	0.25	0.50	1.50	3.00	21*
15,000	0.08	0.38	0.75	2.25	4.50	32*
20,000	0.10	0.50	1.00	3.00	6.00	42*
25,000	0.13	0.63	1.25	3.75	7.50	53*
30,000	0.15	0.75	1.50	4.50	9.00	63*
35,000	0.18	0.88	1.75	5.25	11*	74*
40,000	0.20	1.00	2.00	6.00	12*	84*
50,000	0.25	1.25	2.50	7.50	15*	105*
60,000	0.30	1.50	3.00	9.00	18	126
70,000	0.35	1.75	3.50	10.50	21	147
80,000	0.40	2.00	4.00	12.00	24	168
90,000	0.45	2.25	4.50	13.50	27	189
100,000	0.50	2.50	5.00	15.00	30	210

*Figures of 10.00 or more are expressed to the nearest unit of currency.

The calculations are based on a working year of 238 seven-hour days. If you are self-employed you should make the requisite adjustments for the number of hours and days you work.

at all. And then they wonder afterwards where all the time has gone! That's one of the reasons why it is so important to keep a time log. It is the only way you can know where your time is going.

Work–life balance

From time to time, surveys are published on the attitudes and aspirations of the average worker and citizen. One subject frequently covered is how people regard leisure. When faced with a choice of whether they would prefer to work their present hours for more money or change to a shorter week for less income, a high proportion opt for the extra leisure. In many developed countries, there is a stronger preference for extended vacations, sabbaticals and shorter working weeks or days. Although this does not apply to all categories of workers, certain groups show more interest than others, particularly high-income earners and parents with dual incomes.

Modern living makes greater inroads on our leisure time in a number of different ways, notably:

- The intrusion of government-induced paperwork (tax re- turns, voting rolls, censuses, surveys, etc) and the keeping of accounts and budget planning mean that more people are having to spend more of their leisure time on what may be loosely termed 'life maintenance'. This applies even when they possess a personal computer to help speed up some of these record-keeping processes.
- Many of us are travelling longer distances to work by road or rail and the transport networks are becoming more congested, so more time is spent commuting. That extra time is a loss to the people involved and the economy of the country. These are non-productive and often stress-inducing hours.
- The shortage and increasing cost of reliable workers mean that more people spend more time on essential home decoration, maintenance and improvement. This is a factor that becomes less pleasurable to them and more physically demanding as they grow older.
- Increased prosperity gives us the resources to consume more, and this consumption demands time. The greatly increased stock of consumer goods demands time to acquire and enjoy them. We have time-saving devices which paradoxically demand time for maintenance.
- Large numbers of us use several credit and debit cards. In addition, we may have credit cards from retail outlets, cards for automatic teller machines, frequent-flyer cards, air miles cards, hotel cards, etc. All these generate monthly statements that need reconciliation with receipts and expenditure records.

The time spent in ensuring we receive proper credit or are billed properly will vary with the number of cards we hold, but we are all spending more time on something that was initially designed to save us time. Ironic, isn't it?

■ The ubiquitous mobile phone, e-mail and other technological developments mean that people may be accessible 24/7 irrespective of their location.

Against this background there is a mounting demand from people to enjoy a better quality of life. They want more control of their own lives and more choices in the way they use their time. This is shown in the increasing desire for life-enrichment programmes, flexible time, a variable career pattern and, most of all, the rise in self-employment.

In many countries a growing number of people are becoming cash-rich, time-poor (CRTP), particularly the middle-aged. The CRTP switch from do-it-yourself activities to GAPI (get a person in), assuming they can find a trades person. In the home, the CRTP effect has brought about the re-emergence of servants, although they are no longer so called. They are known as domestics, nannies, au pairs and so on.

It is all the more important that we make more effective use of what limited leisure time we do have at our disposal. The first step in doing this is to make an analysis of where it goes at present. Take a sheet of paper and list down the left-hand side all the aspects of your life in order of their importance to you. This list should include your family, work, friends, holidays, transport, money, fitness, food, clothes, hobbies and so on. On the right-hand side of the same sheet, make an estimate of the amount of time you have devoted to each item on your list during the past month. Compare the priorities against the time spent. Look for those items which are high in priority but low on time spent. Ask yourself what you are going to do about the imbalances. When you have decided what changes you are going to make regarding your allocation of time on the various items, enter the new monthly amounts on your list and enter this in your computer. Run off at least two hard copies, one for home and one for work.

Table 2.2 Time analysis

My life	My last month	Future months
Spouse/partner (and family)		
Job		
Friends		
Money and investments		
Recreation		
Sleep		
Volunteering – community work		
Self-development		
Spirituality		
Other		

Look at your new allocations periodically and make sure you're sticking to them. Table 2.2 illustrates this approach.

How do you spend your non-working time?

Apart from our daily work for a living, which consumes approximately a third of our time, and sleeping, which consumes approximately another third, there are broadly five other practical activities which consume our non-working time. These are:

- Personal needs: washing, shaving, applying and removing make-up, dressing and undressing, eating, etc.
- Travel: commuting, visiting clients, making cold calls, etc.
- Self-improvement: studying, attending courses, reading, body and mind training.
- Domestic responsibilities: shopping, housekeeping, meal preparation, loading and unloading a dishwasher, repairs, gardening, minding children, doing laundry, car and equipment maintenance.
- Recreation: rest, leisure, vacations, hobbies, sport, etc.

While some of the activities that are not work are optional, many are not. Unless you are fortunate enough to work from home, some time is used in commuting. This will vary depending on such things as the distance between home and the workplace, traffic congestion, public transport and weather.

As a first step towards securing increased leisure time, it is useful to make an analysis of the time spent on each of these activity sectors during a typical week, as in Table 2.3.

Table 2.3 Activity–time analysis for a typical week

Day	Work	Sleep	Personal	Commuting, self-improvement, domestic, leisure, etc
Mon				
Tues				
Wed				
Thurs				
Fri				
Subtotal				
Sat				
Sun				
Total				

This analysis may help you to identify some ways to increase your leisure time, albeit at a price in some cases. If you had kept an analysis like this over the years, you might have found that the amount of time spent on personal, self-improvement and leisure activities was continuously decreasing. This is what we refer to as 'optional time': you have the option of how you spend it. With work, commuting and domestic activities you really don't have an option, as you have to do these things. These aspects are probably consuming more of your time at the expense of the others. Better time management will help you find an improved balance between the various activities.

Possible time-saving strategies could include some of the following practical hints:

■ Trying to reschedule your commuting to avoid peak periods (eg making use of flexitime) or finding some better ways of using this captive time (see 'Using your commuting time' and 'Making your sleep work for you', below).

■ Making appointments whenever possible to minimize waiting time. Some waiting is inevitable. Indeed, an enormous amount of our time is consumed in waiting: we wait for appointments, we wait for planes, trains and buses, we wait in the supermarket and at the bank. It is therefore important to devise ways to use waiting time effectively. For example, your visit to the doctor is supposed to be therapeutic, yet for many people the inevitable waiting can be stress-inducing. Accordingly, decide in advance how you want to pass waiting time. If you want to read periodicals, bring your own to avoid disappointment and frustration, or bring work. Any visitors who come through the door are not there to see you. And when the phone rings it's not for you, so you can have productive, uninterrupted time while waiting to be seen by the doctor. You can turn a potentially stress-inducing event into a productive period.

■ Paying as many bills as possible by direct debit, or writing all your cheques at a fixed time each month.

■ Shopping on the internet, by telephone or by mail order.

■ Hiring other people to perform time-consuming tasks.

■ Bartering, ie arranging for a friend to do some tasks distasteful to you but which they enjoy tackling, and doing something you enjoy for them in exchange.

■ Making use of service agencies, eg letting travel agents obtain visas and tickets for you, or paying for service washes at a laundrette.

■ Doubling up on time, eg exercising when watching television, using your sleep time (again, see below).

■ Pooling resources, eg doing the school run on alternate weeks, or on certain days only each week, by arrangement with your friends or neighbours.

- Making greater use of labour-saving devices such as telephone answering machines (whether you are present or not), fax machines, dishwashers.
- Doing your banking by phone or online and using an ATM.

All of us spend time travelling or sleeping, which some people may regard as time wasted. Here are some suggestions for making productive use of time while engaged on these essential functions.

Using your commuting time

Time spent commuting can be analysed. Whether you travel by car or by train, ask yourself such questions as:

- How much time have I spent commuting during the past few months?
- What are the gains from it?
- Are the benefits of commuting worth the time invested in terms of the accomplishments and lifestyle I want most?
- If not, what are the alternatives? Do I have any real choice?
- If commuting is the only answer, am I making best use of my commuting time? When travelling could I:
  - read more?
  - listen to tape recordings?
  - do some paperwork?
  - plan or analyse problems?
  - make phone calls?
  - do some keep-fit exercises?
  - do some memory tests;
  - learn a foreign language?
  - update foreign-language skills?
  - send e-mail and faxes from my laptop computer?
  - do research on the internet?
  - check out useful websites?

- Would the benefits of first-class travel outweigh the extra cost?
- Where flexitime is available, have I chosen my travel times to the best overall advantage?

Making your sleep work for you

There is nothing sacred in sleeping eight hours and keeping awake for 16 hours. The 24-hour day is an accident of astronomy.

Further, sleep may not restore energy when you fall asleep tense and exhausted, as stress toxins may remain in your system. Hence, you may find it better to break up your sleep. If you are sluggish after lunch, try having a nap.

What you eat and drink before retiring can also make a difference. Some nutrients are sleep-inducing. Sleep is not a pause to allow an overheated engine to recover. Rather it is a creative period which allows you to deal with the things not dealt with during the day. Hence, it is often possible to make sleep work for you.

Try these ideas:

- Just before falling asleep, pose some questions to your subconscious. Often, on awakening you may find you have the answers.
- Keep paper and pen or digital voice recorder by your bedside to record any important thoughts in your mind when you wake up.
- Use a timer to turn on taped material you want to learn subliminally.

03

Choosing the way you spend your time

What an uncanny and distressing disproportion appears between the glorious magnitude of that craving and the tiny satisfaction it brings!

Desmond McCarthy

Much of our consumption of time is involuntary: during our formative years we act in accordance with hidden choices made for us by parents and other authority figures – schoolteachers, religious leaders, uncles and aunts, bosses at work. This is part of a very interesting theory by Dr Eric Berne, psychologist and author of the famous book, *Games People Play*, which contains some ideas directly relevant to self- and time management.

According to Berne, these 'parent messages' run through our heads like a recording, consciously or unconsciously, whenever we have a decision to make, and help to shape our values, prejudices, stereotypes and clichés. In consequence, when faced with a choice of what to do with our time, we may be heavily affected by these established patterns, which are extremely difficult to shake off. But shake them off we must, if we are to be truly in command of our own destiny.

In addition, Berne says that there is another part of us which is always acting in a way that earns us 'strokes' – tangible units of recognition. We all have a deep inbuilt hunger for recognition, whether we acknowledge this consciously or not. We can earn strokes legitimately (by doing a job well and gaining appreciation or thanks from others who will benefit from it) or illegitimately (by making a nuisance of ourselves and grabbing attention in other ways). The absence of any recognition at all over a long period is regarded as the worst thing that can happen to a person, who may in the extreme die prematurely of neglect as a result of lack of any human contact. You may remember cases at school or at work of people being 'sent to Coventry', ie being totally ignored. This is regarded as the worst form of punishment that can be inflicted by others.

Time structuring

Because of our need to receive strokes, we consciously or subconsciously structure the time we have at our disposal by engaging in those pursuits that will earn us the kind of strokes for which we are looking (or are prepared to accept if our choices are limited).

Berne describes the principal ways in which we can structure our time in the following six categories:

> **Activities.** He uses this word to describe any constructive, purposeful or creative pursuit in which we may be engaged. This is intended to include our normal work and many types of hobbies such as DIY, gardening, model making or learning to play a musical instrument. Any strokes gained from these are genuine ones that come from a sense of achievement and/or the recognition gained from others.
>
> **Pastimes.** These include competitive games and other kinds of amusements that literally 'pass the time' in a way that gives us pleasure but does not necessarily achieve an end product of lasting value. Any strokes gained here will be at the opponent's expense if the game is won.
>
> **Rituals.** These can cover anything from a greeting or handshake to a cocktail party or major ceremony such as a baptism, confirmation, bar mitzvah, wedding or funeral, when the form of activity is to a large extent prescribed by custom and etiquette. The strokes exchanged during such proceedings are often referred to as 'plastic' ones – not as good as the real thing.
>
> **Withdrawal.** For busy people who need a rest, for people who are shy or unsociable or for those who simply prefer their own company, withdrawal is a way of avoiding the exchange of strokes for a period. It can be achieved by meditating, reading a book, surfing the internet, listening to a CD or going for a walk alone. The main feature of withdrawal is the avoidance of human contact.

Intimacy. This is the situation of complete trust and openness between two or more people where strokes (tangible units of recognition) can be exchanged naturally and without pretence, anxiety or active stroke seeking. These strokes are the best and most satisfying kind but perhaps the hardest to obtain for many people.

Games. For people who feel themselves deprived of strokes, playing games, in Berne's sense of the expression, is the only remaining means of gaining them – albeit illegitimately. It includes any form of interpersonal or political intrigue where the aim is to achieve some covert or secret pay-off at the expense of another person. The strokes are gained by manipulation and usually by 'putting other people down'. In extreme cases, certain game players are prepared to obtain a negative stroke by putting themselves down if it cannot be obtained in any other way. By any orthodox standards, playing such games is a form of paranoia and a sheer waste of time.

Not everybody will readily accept Berne's formulation but it certainly makes us think! How do we spend most of our time? Is it in a hungry quest for strokes as such or is it in activities that are intrinsically worthwhile and will generate genuine strokes as a by-product? Can any of us be completely indifferent to the strokes we receive and those we need?

There is only one way to find out, which is to take a typical week and make an objective analysis of the time we are spending in each of the six categories. Are we satisfied with the result or is there too much ritual behaviour, too much politics or too much withdrawal? There is little lasting satisfaction to be obtained from any of these three categories.

Personal drivers

An extension of Berne's theory says that most of us often fail to enjoy the present moment because we live at the mercy of one or more of the five powerful influences, known as 'drivers', on the following list:

to be perfect;
to try hard;
to please others (or have them please us);
to be in a hurry (the 'time nut');
to be strong.

Most of us have one of these as a primary driver, usually backed up by a secondary one, which helps to make our own life a misery at times. The consequences, both positive and negative, of the five drivers are set out in Table 3.1; any person (and there are some!) who lives at the mercy of all five clearly deserves our sympathy – as indeed does anyone forced to live or work with that person.

Knowledge of our primary driver – which can often be identified from our tone of voice, choice of words, body language, etc – can be helpful in guiding us in how to spend our time more effectively. Once you identify your primary driver you will obtain some valuable knowledge of a factor that may be adversely affecting the effective management of your time. Having done so:

- List all its disadvantages.
- Demonstrate *how* it costs you time.
- Describe any adverse effects it may have on others who live or work with you.
- Decide on some specific changes you could make that would reduce these negative aspects.
- Estimate the time you could save in a week from implementing these changes.
- After you have implemented them, check the results against your estimate. The answer will probably be a pleasant surprise.

This self-analysis will be developed more fully in the next chapter.

Table 3.1 The five personal drivers: advantages and disadvantages

Driver	Advantages	Disadvantages	Questions to ask
Be perfect	Completes a task so that it will not need to be re-done. Plans carefully. Very orderly – items can be found easily.	Spends too much time perfecting work that does not need detailed analysis. Explains at great length. May delay projects by over-planning.	What projects are time being spent on that do not require first-class detailed performance?
Try hard	Loyalty bends every effort to accomplish tasks, even if not quickly.	Takes no short cuts. Makes decisions slowly.	Is it really so hard? What short cuts can be made to get the job finished sooner?
Please others	Accommodates needs of others at own expense. Seeks to create harmony. Saves time for other people.	Time-consuming desire to please everyone. Asks many questions and consults others too often. Leaves own work in favour of others, allows them to eat into own time, then works overtime to catch up.	What must be accomplished today even though nothing is done for others? How can oneself be pleased as well as pleasing others?
Be in a hurry	Does a lot of work in a short time. Excellent on jobs that do not require detail.	Hurries through important work, missing details, causing frequent errors. Work has to be repeated. Doesn't allow time for explanation. Wrong assumptions waste valuable time.	What tasks require fullest attention? When can planning time be found to avoid need for rush?
Be strong	Makes rational, unemotional decisions. Avoids being bothered much by others. Is freer from interruptions than most.	Poor on human relations. Often wastes own and others' valuable time on avoidable staff problems as a result.	Would greater openness with staff avoid the problems? What is the underlying fear that prevents closeness with others?

04

Getting to know yourself better

Nobody knows me better than I know myself. I am a self-sufficient person who doesn't need to be informed by others about my strengths and limitations.

Anonymous

However clear we may be about our goals and our intentions in achieving them, it would be foolish to ignore the fact that the road towards self-improvement will be strewn with difficulties. Our time will slip away unproductively, sometimes without our even realizing it and sometimes with our conscious collusion. We may attempt to blame others for this without appreciating the extent to which it is under our own control. Many of these difficulties arise, in fact, from blocks within ourselves; we may *think* we know our own strengths and weaknesses as in the quotation above, but how do we check our suppositions? How do we discover and remove our own mental blocks? This chapter points your way towards finding out these answers. By doing this you will use your time more effectively and stop wasting the time of others.

To plan your life more effectively and manage your time more efficiently, you need to obtain a better knowledge of yourself and of the effect you have on other people to whom you relate. You need to be able to anticipate more correctly how you are likely to behave in future, as yet unknown, situations. You need to be able to handle fuller self-knowledge, however uncomfortable this may be at the time of revelation, without denying or censoring any information that may be inconsistent with your present self-image. If you are really serious about getting an answer to the question 'What am I really like?' there are several different avenues towards obtaining the necessary knowledge.

Personality tests

Many well-researched tests are in regular use for career coun-selling, team building, job selection, etc. Often these consist of a series of questions which you answer yourself, involving a forced choice between a number of different given replies. Taken together, with professional decoding and interpretation, these can build up a profile of your personality and give an indication of how you are likely to behave in various circumstances. They highlight either your preferences or your strengths and limita-tions, pointing the way towards your future development needs. Good professional tests vary considerably, not only in their com-plexity and purpose but also in the way they are administered. Some of the best-known and most universally applicable tests include the Myers-Briggs, the DiSC and the Platinum Rule, each of which needs to be administered by qualified practitioners. There are plenty of other good tests that do not have this restriction, but beware of making your personality assessment on the cheap by taking too seriously the do-it-yourself 'personality quizzes' that abound in some magazines, online and in popular digests; at best these are likely to be superficial and, at worst, dangerously misleading. It is worth paying the proper price for a professional test; remember: it is *your* life that is at stake. Good tests have high validity, reliability and standardized instructions. It is also important that appropriate norms are used, so that like is being compared with like.

One further point about personality tests: in most cases the profile that emerges comes entirely from data which you orig-inated yourself when you answered the questions. So, however carefully they may be planned, administered and cross-checked, there is always the faint possibility of self-deception through the person who is answering the questions having consciously or unwittingly chosen what appear to be the most 'respectable' of the choices offered. People are often advised to guard against this by answering as spontaneously as possible, and recording the first answer that enters their heads. Some tests have built-in 'lie detectors': they ask the same questions in different ways. Remember the quote from Shakespeare: 'This above all: to thine own self be true, And it must follow as the night the day, Thou canst not then be false to any man.'

An external perception is a valuable corrective to the tendency to self-deception, provided it is relatively free from bias and value judgements. We need to develop contacts with friends and colleagues who will not shirk from giving us their honest assessment of our performance, behaviour and personality as they appear to them. There is a definite art and skill in exchanging feedback of this kind without spoiling the relationship between the two people concerned.

Myers-Briggs Type Indicator (MBTI)

The MBTI was developed by the mother–daughter team of Katherine Briggs and Isabel Briggs Myers. The MBTI is based on the type theory of the famous Swiss psychiatrist Carl Jung.

The MBTI is a self-assessment instrument that determines your preferences on four scales: extroverted or introverted (E or I), sensing or intuitive (S or N), thinking or feeling (T or F) and perceiving or judging (P or J). By completing the instrument you assign yourself to a type, designated by four letters. The MBTI is a tool to uncover the way you prefer to perceive and judge the world and is based on dichotomous items in such a way that scale interactions yield 16 basic personality types. Table 4.1 shows the 16 different personality types.

Personal Profile System (DiSC)

This instrument also helps you to understand yourself through identifying your behavioural profile and the environment most conducive to your success. You are given 28 groups of four words. You are requested to select the word that most describes you and the one that least describes you in each group.

The reason the instrument is also known as DiSC is because it zooms in on the following four dimensions of behaviour: dominance, influence, conscientiousness and steadiness.

With dominance, the emphasis is on shaping the environment by overcoming opposition to accomplish results. This person's tendencies include:

- getting immediate results;
- causing action;
- accepting challenges;
- making quick decisions;
- questioning the status quo;
- taking authority;
- managing trouble;
- solving problems.

With influence, the emphasis is on shaping the environment by influencing or persuading others. This person's tendencies include:

- contacting people;
- making a favourable impression;
- speaking articulately;
- creating a motivational environment;
- generating enthusiasm;
- entertaining people;
- viewing people and situations optimistically;
- participating in a group.

With conscientiousness, the emphasis is on working conscientiously within existing circumstances to ensure quality and accuracy. This person's tendencies include:

- attention to key directives and standards;
- concentrating on key details;
- thinking analytically, weighing pros and cons;
- being diplomatic with people;
- using subtle or indirect approaches to conflict;

Table 4.1 The 16 different personality types

| | | Sensing types (S) | | Intuitive types (N) | |
		Thinking (T)	Feeling (F)	Feeling (F)	Thinking (T)
Introverts	Judging	**ISTJ** Serious, quiet, earn success by concentration and thoroughness. Practical, orderly, matter-of-fact, logical, realistic and dependable. Take responsibility.	**ISFJ** Quiet, friendly, responsible and conscientious. Work devotedly to meet their obligations. Thorough, painstaking, accurate. Loyal, considerate.	**INFJ** Succeed by perseverance, originality and desire to do whatever is needed or wanted. Quietly forceful, conscientious, concerned for others. Respected for their firm principles.	**INTJ** Usually have original minds and great drive for their own ideas and purposes. Sceptical, critical, independent, determined, often stubborn.
	Perceiving	**ISTP** Cool onlookers – quiet, reserved and analytical. Usually interested in impersonal principles, how and why mechanical things work. Flashes of original humour.	**ISFP** Retiring, quietly friendly, sensitive, kind, modest about their abilities. Shun disagreements. Loyal followers. Often relaxed about getting things done.	**INFP** Care about learning, ideas, language and independent projects of their own. Tend to undertake too much, then somehow get it done. Friendly, but often too absorbed.	**INTP** Quiet, reserved, impersonal. Enjoy theoretical or scientific subjects. Usually interested mainly in ideas, little liking for parties or small talk. Sharply defined interests.

Extroverts				
Perceiving	**ESTP** Matter-of-fact, do not worry or hurry, enjoy whatever comes along. May be a bit blunt or insensitive. Best with real things that can be taken apart or put together.	**ESFP** Outgoing, easygoing, accepting, friendly, make things more fun for others by their enjoyment. Like sports and making things. Find remembering facts easier than mastering theories.	**ENFP** Warmly enthusiastic, high-spirited, ingenious, imaginative. Able to do almost anything that interests them. Quick with a solution and to help with a problem.	**ENTP** Quick, ingenious, good at many things. May argue either side of a question for fun. Resourceful in solving challenging problems, but may neglect routine assignments.
Judging	**ESTJ** Practical, realistic, matter-of-fact, with a natural head for business or mechanics. Not interested in subjects they see no use for. Like to organize and run activities.	**ESFJ** Warm-hearted, talkative, popular, conscientious, born cooperators. Need harmony. Work best with encouragement. Little interest in abstract thinking or technical subjects.	**ENFJ** Responsive and responsible. Generally feel real concern for what others think or want. Sociable, popular. Sensitive to praise and criticism.	**ENTJ** Hearty, frank, decisive leaders. Usually good in anything that requires reasoning and intelligent talk. May sometimes be more positive than their experience in an area warrants.

- checking for accuracy;
- analysing performance critically;
- using a systematic approach to situations or activities.

With steadiness, the emphasis is on cooperating with others to carry out the task. This person's tendencies include:

- performing in a consistent, predictable manner;
- demonstrating patience;
- developing specialized skills;
- desiring to help others;
- showing loyalty;
- being a good listener;
- calming excited people;
- creating a stable, harmonious work environment.

The Platinum Rule

According to its workbook, The Platinum Rule will teach you to understand that many behaviours can be positioned within a systematic, predictable framework. Identify how a person's behavioural patterns influence what that person wants, needs and expects from you and others, and how the person communicates this. It will also teach you how to adapt effectively to people.

The Platinum Rule is based on the premise that a person's behaviour can be classified on two dimensions: openness and directness. It defines openness as 'the readiness and willingness with which a person outwardly shows emotions or feelings and develops interpersonal relationships', and directness as 'the amount of control and forcefulness a person attempts to exercise over situations or other's thoughts and emotions'.

The following are the open behaviours provided in the workbook:

- self-disclosing;
- shows and shares feelings freely;

- makes most decisions based on feelings (subjective);
- conversation includes digressions; strays from the subject;
- relaxed and warm;
- goes with the flow;
- opinion- and feeling-oriented;
- easy to get to know in business or unfamiliar social situations;
- flexible about how their time is used by others;
- prefers to work with others;
- initiates/accepts physical contact;
- shares, or enjoys listening to, personal feelings, especially if positive;
- animated facial expressions during speaking and listening;
- shows more enthusiasm than the average person;
- friendly handshake;
- more likely to give non-verbal feedback;
- responsive to dreams/visions/concepts.

The following list is provided for self-contained behaviours:

- guarded;
- keeps feelings private: shares only on a 'need-to-know' basis;
- makes most decisions based on evidence (objective);
- focuses conversation on issues and tasks; stays on the subject;
- more formal and proper;
- goes with the agenda;
- fact- and task-oriented;
- takes time to get to know in business or unfamiliar social situations;
- disciplined about how their time is used by others;
- prefers to work independently;
- avoids/minimizes physical contact;
- tells, or enjoys listening to, goal-oriented stories and anecdotes;
- limited range of facial expressions during speaking and listening;
- shows less enthusiasm than the average person;
- formal handshake;

- less likely to give non-verbal feedback, if they give it at all;
- responsive to realities/actual experiences/facts.

The workbook provides the following examples of indirect behaviours:

- approaches risk, decision or change slowly/cautiously;
- infrequent contributor to group conversations;
- infrequent use of gestures and voice intonation to emphasize points;
- often makes qualified statements: 'According to my sources...', 'I think so';
- emphasizes points through explanations of the content of the message;
- questions tend to be for clarification/support/information;
- reserves expression of opinions;
- more patient and cooperative;
- diplomatic;
- when not in agreement (if it's no big deal), most likely to go along;
- understated; reserved;
- initial eye contact is intermittent;
- at social gathering, more likely to wait for others to introduce themselves;
- gentle handshake;
- tends to follow established rules and policies.

And a list of direct behaviours:

- approaches risk, decisions or change quickly/spontaneously;
- frequent contributor to group conversations;
- frequently uses gestures and voice intonation to emphasize points;
- often makes emphatic statements: 'This is so!', 'I'm positive!';
- emphasizes points through confident vocal intonation and assertive body language;

- questions tend to be rhetorical, to emphasize points or to challenge information;
- expresses opinions readily;
- less patient; competitive;
- confronting;
- more likely to maintain their position when not in agreement (argue);
- intense, assertive;
- initial eye contact is sustained;
- more likely to introduce self to others at social gathering;
- firm handshake;
- tends to bend/break established rules and policies.

The open and self-contained, direct and indirect types of behaviour lead in combinations to four styles that reflect the following generalized character types: socializer, director, thinker and relater.

05

Avoiding procrastination, the time thief

> I have been meaning for some time to set up a national association of procrastinators, but I just haven't got around to it yet.

Anonymous

The above statement is typical of a certain weakness that we all indulge in from time to time. Procrastination – the habit of putting things off or doing low-priority tasks or actions rather than higher-priority ones – is a widespread time-wasting practice and can be very costly. For example, procrastination may lead to:

- external consequences ranging from the comparatively innocuous (charges arising from the failure to pay a credit card statement on time) to something potentially very serious (loss of one's job);
- internal consequences that may range from mild irritation with oneself to extreme dissatisfaction and unhappiness.

Not all postponement is procrastination; sometimes there are perfectly valid and positive reasons for not rushing into a decision today when you know it makes more sense to devote tomorrow to considering it more thoroughly. If a job can legitimately wait, has low priority or is awaiting information that will improve the quality of the eventual decision, there may be every reason for taking no action for the time being. Sometimes a problem may even resolve itself if left. Good management practice includes knowing when, and for how long, to leave things alone. Sometimes the most rational decision is 'no action'.

But this is by no means always the case. Procrastination has a large element of irrationality about it. We put off dealing with difficult things because we just cannot be bothered with them now or because we have more interesting things with which to occupy ourselves. We involve ourselves in low-priority tasks today and put off the higher-priority ones indefinitely for reasons that we cannot logically defend – maybe for fear of the consequences. Procrastination is a decision not to decide, or a decision by default. It is related to incompetence and inefficiency.

Some excuses for procrastination

A year from now, will it really matter that I didn't do it?
If I wait long enough, the boss will forget about it.
If I do it, I will only be wrong.
It's too late in the week/day to start it now.
I'll wait till I'm in the mood to do it.
I've been working hard, I deserve a break.
I haven't got the right tools for the job.

It was said of the editor of one newspaper famed for his indecisiveness, 'The editor's indecision is final.'

How people procrastinate

Having to make decisions may cause considerable stress, which leads to the development of numerous effective decision-avoidance techniques. These include:

- Appointing a committee to delay decision making. One definition of a committee is a group of people who individually prefer to do nothing and who meet collectively so that nothing can be done.
- Seeking clarification by asking:
  - for more details;
  - the reason for wishing to change;
  - the consequence of change.

This analysis-paralysis method can delay the decision requested, often with damaging consequences.

- Using the denial method: denying that a decision has to be made.
- Confusing the issue.
- Confusing the request, in particular by the use of jargon or 'doublespeak'.
- Handing back the problem: telling the requester that the problem is theirs, not yours.

Some reasons why people procrastinate

Procrastination can be traced to a variety of causes including:

- Avoiding unpleasant tasks. There is a paradox about this. When procrastination stems from a desire to avoid doing something unpleasant that might prove critical, the procrastination itself will probably increase the unpleasantness, since the job still has to be done. Furthermore, failure to act may generate problems not just for oneself but also for others.

  Counting the cost of delay may help to get things moving. If tempted to procrastinate, ask yourself, 'What problems am I likely to create for myself?' And if you don't want to live with those problems, don't procrastinate!

  Irrespective of the approach adopted, before starting a job give some thought to the environment. Ensure that there are no distractions, such as the telephone or visitors. On completion of the work, reward yourself. The size of the reward can be related to the size of the task – from a coffee break to that golfing weekend you've been promising yourself.

- Avoiding difficult tasks. Sometimes tasks are not tackled because the person responsible may find them too demanding. In which case:
  - It may be possible to break the task down into subunits that can be handled effectively.
  - It may be desirable to spend some time considering the subject before attempting the task, or asking someone

to assist you in learning the job. Many unfamiliar things appear to be difficult, but are not really so at all.
- Begin the task during a period of prime time when you are feeling at a high point both mentally and physically.
- Check that standards are not set too high, for perfectionism may not be justifiable or necessary.

■ Fear of making a mistake. This may arise from yourself. Those of us who suffer from fear of making a mistake should keep a 'worry list' of things we fear may go wrong. Periodically check how many went right. As a rule it will be found that in fact things did not go wrong; when you are armed with such knowledge, confidence will develop. Build upon this. A decision should not be looked upon as a problem; rather it should be seen as an opportunity.

Fear of making a mistake often causes procrastination until all the facts are available; yet in many instances delaying the decision will add little, if anything, to its quality.

Alternatively, procrastination may arise because of others. Managers (and parents) may push for perfection from their direct reports (or children) and anything falling short is punished. When this happens, perfection is less likely to be achieved because the situation generates anxiety and stress which, in turn, result in less than the best ensuing.

■ Habit. If people are allowed to put things off, this can become a habit. Procrastination breeds procrastination. The behaviour is reinforced. To generate a 'never put off till tomorrow what can be done today' mentality may require a programme of positive action aimed at building up good habits. The development of good habits does not change the task, but it will certainly change a person's attitude and perception.

In replacing old habits with new ones, you should:
- pinpoint what you wish to change, but don't try to change too much at one time;
- devise a new routine to replace the old;
- set clear and challenging performance targets;
- make the change immediately;
- launch the new habit with strength and commitment;
- announce the change publicly;

- practise the new habit without exception until it is firmly rooted;
- recognize that it may take time and practice to ensure the desired results.

There are some further subconscious reasons why people become chronic procrastinators:

- to enjoy exercising power over people;
- to avoid getting close to people's personal problems;
- to avoid being held responsible;
- or just laziness!

Excitement

Some people put off doing things until the last moment because they find it exciting to face tight deadlines. Linked with this may be how they wish to be seen by others – for example, as people who are overworked, wrestling under pressure but managing to meet the deadline – although whether their last-minute report will be as good as one started much earlier may be another matter.

Some ways to avoid or correct procrastination

The most effective way to handle unpleasant tasks is to schedule them for the beginning of the day. Where this is not possible, then a deadline for beginning the tasks should be set. The pressure of a deadline serves as a stimulant to action. If necessary, let other people know about the deadline, since breaking commitments then becomes more embarrassing. It is also relevant to remind ourselves that when the going gets tough, the tough get going.

If the task seems too complex to tackle all at once, use what Alan Lakein has called the 'Swiss cheese' technique, ie making a few holes in it to start with, by doing the easy bits first and working outwards from each point of entry so that the holes gradually become larger and meet one another.

Alternatively, you can use the 'divide and conquer' principle, which breaks a large job into smaller chunks and demolishes one chunk at each sitting. This is sometimes likened to devouring an elephant slice by slice.

With these methods you can take advantage of any five- or ten-minute intervals in your other engagements to get a preview of the next instalment, so that you are better equipped mentally for your next scheduled start. If possible, try to involve somebody else in doing the bits that you feel ill equipped to do yourself (see Chapter 18). In this way the job can be going ahead even while you are otherwise engaged. If you must tackle it alone, always try to do so at one of your prime-time periods (see Chapter 7) when you know you will be mentally and physically at your peak.

Schedule your worry time

Schedule your worry time: say, 5 pm each Thursday. By then you will find a very high proportion of your worries will have solved themselves.

If you are one of those people who live in fear of making a mistake, examine your own standards to see whether you have perhaps set them too high for the particular job in hand. Perfectionists should remember the saying, 'The best is often the enemy of the good,' and realize that it can be a costly mistake to provide a Rolls-Royce in a few weeks' time for a customer who is looking for a Volkswagen now.

The Pareto principle: the vital few and the trivial many

The Pareto principle states that 80 per cent of most jobs can be accomplished with only 20 per cent of the available effort, and that it is the remaining 20 per cent of the job that makes the heaviest inroads on our time and energy. Ask yourself whether it is this remaining 20 per cent (ie putting the gloss on the job) that is really the cause of your delayed start, and you could probably knock off the first 80 per cent in next to no time. Is the extra 20 per cent really worth the worry?

Innumerable examples can be found of the 80/20 distribution in many walks of life, especially business. For example:

- 80 per cent of sales are often earned by 20 per cent of a firm's products;
- 80 per cent of revenue (or of complaints) may come from 20 per cent of the customers (not usually the *same* 20 per cent for both!);
- 80 per cent of telephone calls are made by 20 per cent of subscribers;
- 80 per cent of total sick leave is taken by 20 per cent of a company's employees;
- 80 per cent of total viewing time is spent watching the 20 per cent most popular programmes.

The principle is named after the Italian economist Vilfredo Pareto, who identified it in the 19th century while studying the distribution of wealth in various societies. In nearly all the cases he examined the 'significant few' who owned 80 per cent of the available wealth numbered only 20 per cent of the population.

It is quite easy to identify fields in which this 80/20 rule applies. (Sometimes the percentages may be a little more or a little less, but the 80/20 rule can be relied on to be correct 80 per cent of the time!) If you are in any doubt, you can create a cumulative graph of frequency versus volume to test it. For example, you may suspect that a high proportion of a company's sales revenue is recorded on a small proportion of ledger cards; in which case the cards can be listed in descending order of value, showing cumulative revenue and percentage of total revenue, and the results plotted on a graph.

A typical Pareto distribution would show:

- about 20 per cent of really significant items;
- perhaps another 30 per cent having some significance;
- the remainder of negligible significance.

The items can then be coded A, B and C, and handled in the following way in future:

- A items should be handled in detail and tightly controlled;
- B items should be handled with some respect;
- C items should be dealt with as expeditiously and economically as possible, eg using sampling methods for control.

In practice there is far too much pressure for uniformity, and an unnecessary amount of time is devoted to detailed checking of trivia. A more intelligent approach, in terms of the vital effect on the bottom line, is to concentrate major time and effort on the significant few.

Are you a procrastinator?

Many of us do not fully know the extent of our procrastination. Nor may the procrastination range over every facet of our behaviour. For example, try compiling a checklist of activities covering:

- work;
- household;
- personal care;
- social relationships.

It may emerge that you procrastinate selectively, while in some cases it may be difficult to distinguish between procrastinating and doing something for pleasure. Reading a newspaper or journal may be procrastination or something you are doing for pleasure.

When you say 'I should,' do you mean 'I don't want to'?

When you say 'I can't,' 'I might,' or 'I'll try,' do you mean 'I won't'?

When you say 'I don't have time,' do you mean 'I'm not willing to take the time'?

When you say 'I'll get to that shortly,' do you mean 'I'm not willing to set a deadline for myself'?

When you say 'I want to manage my time better,' do you mean 'I'll start tomorrow'?

Or do you think you should really answer these questions some other time?

A manager who repeatedly procrastinates may become interruption-prone because they subconsciously welcome interruptions as a way of putting off the 'evil hour' when they must take an important decision. In other cases procrastination may be reflected in over-involvement in detail, concentrating on minutiae and general disorganization. The extent of the contents of the pending tray on your desk or of the electronic 'to do' file on your computer is usually a good indicator of a tendency towards procrastination. Have a look in your pending tray. Those of us who repeatedly put things off should ask ourselves, 'What am I trying to avoid?'

For a more thorough examination of your own tendency to procrastinate, there is a procrastination analysis that you can try on yourself right now:

1 Make a list of all the tasks on which you are currently delaying taking action or decisions. Have a look in your pending tray.
2 Against each item, write down the reasons why you have not already taken action.
3 Ask yourself if these reasons could justify the delay to another person, or whether they are merely excuses you are making to yourself.
4 Now make a list of any other tasks on which you can recall having procrastinated in the past.
5 Re-examine both lists and see if any pattern emerges. Are there any particular types of task that you repeatedly avoid? Is there anything you would like to do to correct these tendencies?

Living and working with procrastinators

Many of us have to spend time working with procrastinators, or watching those for whom we care facing possible problems because of the manner in which they procrastinate. Ways to assist the procrastinator include:

- Avoid doing certain things such as:
  - Doing the task yourself for the procrastinator. This only reinforces their procrastination. You may further alienate the procrastinator by showing a lack of confidence in their ability.
  - Nagging. It may result in resentment.
  - Using criticism or threats. Momentary compliance may result, but resentment and alienation are the more likely ultimate consequence.
  - Saying 'Just do it.' This may cause the procrastinator to rebel directly or indirectly.
- Discuss the problem with the procrastinator and mutually agree specific deadlines and consequences. If necessary, put these in writing. If the procrastinator will not discuss the situation, only then make a unilateral decision, and ensure that the consequences can be enforced.
- Help the procrastinator. Ways to do this include:
  - Help them to set interim goals. Goal achievement is a motivator.
  - Respond to their performance. Reward progress along the way.
  - Use intangible rewards such as a smile, a nod, a word of encouragement.
  - Always seek to be positive.

Initially you have to invest time in assisting the procrastinators, but once they have developed good habits you secure a return on your investment.

When decision making is by committee, the selection of those involved may be crucial. Aim for the right mixture of thinkers and doers.

Some practical hints

Keep a list of all the tasks you have in hand at any one time. This should show date received, date for review, action taken.

Identify those tasks that for one reason or another you are putting off, doing inadequately or leaving half finished.

Ask yourself why you are failing to clear them. Could they be delegated or broken into sub-tasks?

Think about the consequences for you of further procrastination.

Make a firm decision as to which task you will do next. Or take a gamble: write each one on a separate slip of paper, fold and put them all in a hat; then take them out one at a time and number them in that order for tackling.

Establish daily progress goals for each job you tackle, and don't stop until you have attained them. If this means working extra time at first, it will soon teach you to set more realistic goals to avoid this happening on future occasions.

Promise yourself a small reward for each task completed and then ensure that you earn it.

Ask yourself periodically, 'What is the most productive use to which my time could be put right now?' If the answer is other than what you are doing at that moment, take steps to get to work on the more important task.

Above all, if procrastination really is your problem don't put off tackling it!

06

Removing barriers to your time effectiveness

'I see no ships. I have a right to be blind sometimes; I really do not see the signal.

Admiral Lord Nelson

Facing up to your mental set

People are more likely to perceive what they *expect* to hear or see. For example, if you are expecting a telephone call from someone, you are more likely to recognize their voice when you receive the call; conversely, with an unexpected call, you are less likely to recognize the caller, even though the voice may be well known to you. This tendency to react in a certain way to a given stimulus is termed 'mental set'.

Most medical doctors realize the importance of this phenomenon in relation to sickness or health. They know from experience that patients who regard themselves as prone to sickness are more likely to get sick, whereas those who are predisposed to recovery may well cure themselves without any treatment. Patients given placebos will often recover as quickly as those given drugs, because they are induced to believe that the 'remedy' will effect a cure.

Magicians are another group who rely heavily on mental set; their audiences are led to believe that the magician is doing one thing, such as burning a currency note, when in fact something quite different is really happening unnoticed.

Mental set can have both positive and negative consequences; an example of negative consequence is that you invariably recognize the postman or postwoman when they appear daily on your doorstep, but fail to do so when they appear out of uniform and out of context, eg if you happen to meet them during a shopping trip or on holiday abroad. An example in working life occurs when a sales rep is given a target number of customers to visit within a certain period; the rep may concentrate on maximizing the number of visits in order to attain the target, yet fail to turn any of them into genuine sales opportunities: their mind had become attuned to the wrong objective.

The following two examples illustrate how readily we can all succumb to blinkered thinking because of our mental set and our reluctance to stray from familiar thought patterns. The first is probably familiar as a creativity exercise. It consists of putting nine dots in the form of a square on a piece of paper (see Figure 6.1) and asking another person to link them with four straight lines, without lifting their pen or pencil or going over any line.

Figure 6.1 The nine dot puzzle

Sometimes when faced with this problem those who cannot find the answer get quite defensive when the solution is revealed; they may even regard the solution as some form of cheating (we reveal the solution later in this chapter!). In fact, if the prior assumptions they bring to the problem are relaxed, solutions can be found using only three lines or even just one.

Faced with an unfamiliar situation, most people tend to be drawn by their past experience towards the most likely or most familiar solution rather than approaching it with a completely open mind. This is fine as long as it meets the desired objective; but in these times of unpredictability and constant change, such thinking frequently results in failure to reach a solution at all because we are hidebound by real or imagined rules based on our past experience and consequent expectations. It is probably better practice nowadays to assume that no rules exist unless it is patently clear that they do. Even then we should not let them go unchallenged.

To illustrate the point further, here is the second conundrum. The police break into a locked flat. They find Peter and Mary dead on the floor. Both are naked and lying in a pool of water. There is broken glass on the floor and the window is open. What has happened?

Most people, because of their mental set, automatically start from the assumption that Peter and Mary are human beings. But in this case, Peter and Mary are two goldfish, which of course are always 'naked'. A gust of wind blew through an open window and toppled the fishbowl, shattering it on the floor. (It would be inappropriate to use this as an example in cultures where fish are not kept as pets or are not called by human names. This might actually be offensive, and indeed we apologize if any of our readers take exception to this example.)

Mental set has a profound effect on the way we perceive other people. If we have an argument with somebody, we are more prone to noticing that person's bad points – particularly if we lose the argument. Consequently, whenever an *us* and *them* conflict situation arises, a great deal of time can be wasted. Hence it is more effective in terms of time management to use our time in search of win/win solutions rather than being driven by the over-competitive win/lose atmosphere prevalent in so many organizations.

Invest time to save time

You may find that major payback can ensue from a few creative exercises. As an example, for each of the following, generate five ideas to assist you in using your time more effectively:

- How can you handle your paperwork more effectively?
- How can you handle commuting time effectively?
- How can you reduce the volume of junk e-mail?

Mental set and your job choices

Despite its downside, mental set can be a powerful ally when used positively. For example, if you set your mind sufficiently strongly on achieving a desired objective, you become alerted to various opportunities for working towards the winning post, and your powers of endurance increase accordingly, as many a successful athlete will testify.

Mental set can also have a powerful influence on how you perceive your job. According to Rosemary Stewart of Templeton College, Oxford, a specialist in organizational behaviour, any managerial job can be analysed in terms of three factors:

Demands. These are the things the job holder must do. They may include:
  - obligatory parts of the job, eg preparing a budget;
  - sanctions imposed by the boss, team members or colleagues;
  - aspects of the job that must be done to facilitate doing other obligatory parts, eg attending a meeting.

Constraints. These are the things that proscribe what the job holder cannot do because of government regulations or by-laws, trade union agreements, technological limitations or organizational processes, procedures or regularities.

Choices. These are the options the job holder may exercise.

Hence a person's time may be divided into two parts: the time that cannot be controlled, and the time that can be controlled.

For many jobs there is a much wider range of choice in how they will be performed than incumbents are apt to realize. As evidence of this, observe how holders of similar jobs, or successive incumbents of the same job, will tend to see different aspects of it as being:

very important;
appealing to them;
ones they are better able to do.

Effectiveness is influenced by the nature of the choices that are made. But too often people do not recognize that choices are open to them. Further, there is a key difference in approach between the person who sees the job primarily as responding to and coping with problems and requests as they arise, and another person who sees it as operating in an environment inside and outside which they seek to control, develop and mould as they desire.

The issue of choice has grown increasingly important because the command-and-control structure in many organizations has changed profoundly due to information technology. The availability of information enables people to make decisions for themselves instead of just taking orders from above.

Managers who still work in highly formalized organizations do have some freedom, both to use their own personal style in internal and external relationships and to choose their own working methods.

Similarly, many managerial jobs provide a wider choice of personal starting and finishing times than is sometimes recognized. For example, Rosemary Stewart found that the bank branch managers she studied, all working for the same bank, variously quantified the number of evenings they had to be out at business meetings or dinners from one or two *per month* to two or three *per week*. Such variations are unlikely to be wholly explained in terms of differing local social demands; so the managers concerned must have exercised a considerable element of choice.

There is also some individual choice to be exercised in most managerial jobs over the amount of time devoted to discussion. Talking with one other person tends to be different in character from talking to several people at once. So do you spend your time seeing each person separately or do you see people together when the same topic is under discussion? Your choice can considerably influence the time at your disposal.

A person's approach to their job may be seen as a continuum stretching from proactive, in which they are constantly setting up opportunities to achieve aims, to reactive, which amounts to not much more than a short-term coping with crises or extinguishing fires.

So ask yourself what constraints are hindering the effectiveness of your work or that of your unit, and which ones you can or should try to alter.

It is also worth remembering that it is not important if you come in early and leave late. Why? Because it is not the hours you put in that count; it is what you put into the hours.

Prioritizing your tasks

While choices are undoubtedly important for managerial effectiveness, the first concern of any job holder is to identify those activities that have to be undertaken because no one else is responsible for dealing with them. Choose your activities on the basis of those that are important to the enterprise or for which you have special expertise.

Here is a useful exercise to release people from the feeling of being pressed for time:

1   Take two pieces of paper.
2   Head one of them *Have to do* and the other *Should do.*
3   List on the *Have to do* sheet only those things that must be done today.
4   List on the *Should do* sheet those things that you feel ought to be done sooner or later.
5   File the *Should do* sheet for future reference.
6   Work through the items on the *Have to do* list one by one, in order of priority.

It is essential to be severe in the selection of *Have to do* items; it is surprising how few things you really have to do. A useful test to determine whether something should appear on the *Have to do* list is answering yes to the question, 'Will my work, my co-workers, or my family suffer if I fail to do this today?'

Review the *Should do* list periodically, starting the next day. Later inspection often reveals how inconsequential many of the items are; it is surprising how what seems urgent or important today becomes rapidly outdated by events and pales into insignificance tomorrow.

Mastering your mental set

There is a key difference in approach between managers who see their job as primarily responding to and coping with demands and requests from others as they arise (reactive) and those who believe in making things happen (proactive). If you have any doubts about where you stand, it can be a salutary exercise to answer the following questions:

If I had only half the time I have now, how would I spend it?
If I had total job security, could I start or finish my working day at noon and would I do so?
Am I satisfied with the way I spend my time at present?

It is also worth remembering that regularly coming into work early and staying late is not necessarily a sign of good management; in fact, the converse might well be true. The real point is, why do you do it and what does it achieve for you? Does it really improve your effectiveness or is it merely a greater amount of activity towards achieving the same or even fewer results? If the latter is the case, you may be a victim of that notorious time waster, the activity trap. It is time you realized that your true managerial effectiveness is measured not by your level of activity, your input *effort*, but by your output *results*. In turn, these are influenced by the nature of the conscious choices you make.

All too often managers do not realize that choices are open to them; their mental set invents artificial boundaries and constraints that are not really there at all. They blame their failures on the lack of any options, without realizing that the choices they make are unconsciously developed from past habits and experiences. Their negative mental set is so strong that they simply do not see the more creative solutions open to them. Let us hope that we do not fall into their trap; mental set is a splendid servant but a very poor master.

Encourage out-of-the-box thinking

One solution to the problem in Figure 6.1 is given in Figure 6.2.

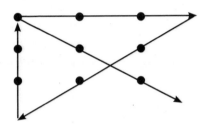

Figure 6.2 Thinking out of the box

Although the task can be done perfectly easily, many people are unable to solve it because their mental set restricts them from going beyond the boundaries of the square, and they fail to see that there is nothing sacrosanct or limiting about its four sides. In other words, what we referred to earlier as their prior assumptions – their mental set – have blocked them from seeing a viable answer.

For many people, recent changes in working practice will make it increasingly difficult to break out of the box. Witness the growth in home working and telecommuting; those involved in this have less opportunity to engage in the friction of fine minds that could contribute to breaking out of their mental set.

Downsizing, re-engineering and changes in lunching habits are also impacting on the likelihood of change. According to a survey by the National Restaurant Association in America, nearly 40 per cent of US workers no longer take a lunch break. Formerly a high proportion would have eaten with colleagues, often in a leisurely fashion; chatting together could frequently have been thought-provoking and impacted favourably on their mental set.

And according to the American office furniture giant, Steelcase, the lunch hour, even among those taking lunch, is nowadays nowhere near an hour – it's a 35-minute stint. More than half the workers taking a lunch break don't actually eat anything. Instead they make personal phone calls, use the time to go shopping, do personal errands, checks on their kids in day care.

Some organizations are aware of the importance of those 'empty spaces of time' in the coffee breaks and lunches when a great deal of creative thinking takes place. So measures are being taken to recreate them. For example, Lord Stone, when joint managing director of Marks & Spencer, often arranged dinner parties with other managers in the company with no purpose other than to talk about life.

Similarly, Gordon McGovern, when chairman of the Campbell Soup Company, held board meetings in the back room of a super-market. Afterwards the participants roamed the aisles seeking comments from shoppers about the company's products.

07

Exploiting your prime time

> I've learned how to manage my energy – I used to just focus on managing my time.
>
> A G Lately, President and CEO, Procter and Gamble

The least productive hours of the working day are the regular working hours, according to a survey by the Omega Watch Corporation. At first sight this may seem nonsensical; but the survey carried out among 100 chief executives of some of the top 500 US companies showed that the majority of them did their most productive work before 9 am (43 per cent), after 5 pm (18 per cent) or during the official lunch hour (5 per cent). On reflection the reason is not hard to find – there were fewer people around at these times to disturb their thinking. Of the remaining 34 per cent who found that they did their best work within the 9 am to 5 pm official day, three out of four said that the mornings were more productive than the afternoons.

Figures like these reflect the fact that many of us have a personal capability pattern that is related to the time of day at which we are working. We each have our 'prime time', when we know from experience that our concentration is at its sharpest, and our 'trough periods', when we achieve very little. At any point in the day our capability pattern may vary between the following recognizable levels:

high energy state	normal working level	just above sleep
quick-witted	relaxed	

Harnessing your natural energy cycle

Broadly speaking, people can be divided into three types in terms of energy levels during the day. These are:

'larks' who rise at dawn and busy themselves straightaway but then fade towards evening;

'owls' who are still asleep (or very near it) in the early part of the day but become more active as the evening approaches and will carry on working or playing all night if necessary;

'fowls' who scratch around all day without experiencing any particular peaks or troughs.

When is your personal prime time? Is your concentration at its sharpest first thing in the morning, late at night or at some other point in the day? To achieve maximum effectiveness, you should, if possible, schedule your tasks so that they match your capability level. When there is a serious mismatch your efficiency will suffer. If the task in hand is below your current capability level, boredom will set in; if a task requiring maximum concentration coincides with one of your low points, frustration will occur.

Are you an am or a pm person?

If you don't already know your prime time, on a non-working day jog or have a brisk walk for five minutes in the morning, middle morning, middle afternoon and late afternoon. The one that leaves you feeling most invigorated is your prime time.

Some of us have internal prime time: when we are at our best working alone and concentrating. Others have an external prime time: when we work best with others.

To get the best from each day, start by plotting a graph of your known energy pattern as it typically varies throughout the day, as shown in Figure 7.1:

1 Plot dots to indicate your relative energy levels at different times during a typical day, with particular reference to the highest and lowest levels.
2 Draw a connecting line between the dots to trace your daily energy cycle or profile.
3 How does this cycle relate to your regular work schedule? Do the most creative or taxing tasks coincide with your high energy points?
4 In what ways could you rearrange your work schedule to take better advantage of your high-energy periods of prime time?

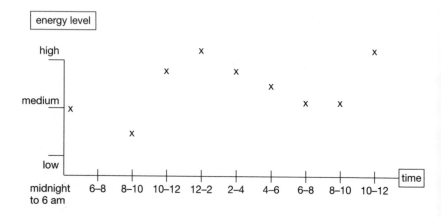

Figure 7.1 Daily energy cycle

For a high proportion of people, the longer they work, the more fatigued they become. This results in reduced productivity. Consequently, if the task must be finished before work can stop, this will mean working for even longer per unit of output. This is a costly and ineffective use of time. In particular, it is senseless to continue working without some kind of a break: energy decreases, physical stress and tension accumulate, mistakes and accidents occur. It is often more productive to take a short break before resuming with renewed effort. A change of pace is often as good as a complete stop: switching from a mental task to a physical one or vice versa can sometimes produce the desired energy top-up. If there is no time for anything more, try isometric exercises: a short walk, one or two knee-bends, a few deep breaths; or just stand up, turn around and sit down again.

If you need some information from another room to complete a written task, go and collect it yourself rather than having it brought to you; the exercise will restore your energy.

Managing the sleepy period after lunch

Some employers actively encourage this, and provide nap rooms and massage recliners. This can boost the productivity of older workers or those with, for example, bad backs, or young parents who have had sleepless nights.

Many people have a sluggish period immediately after lunch, when the body feels it should sleep for a while. Biologists claim that this is due to a low glucose level in the blood while the body is in a state of digestion. The best way to counteract the lulls may be by taking a short nap. Again, some employers actively encourage this. The duration of the sleep should be limited: if you sleep for longer than 20 minutes you enter a deeper sleep and can feel very groggy on awakening. An alternative can be a neck massage at your desk.

Another strategy is to polish off quickly half a dozen minor and less demanding jobs. The resultant sense of achievement can get the adrenalin flowing. Alternatively, if the thought of starting a major task immediately after lunch appears daunting, it may pay to make a start on it before lunch. The satisfaction of completing it more quickly after lunch can be a stimulus. Likewise, if you have a few minutes following the completion of a big job before leaving for lunch, the time can profitably be used to assemble some of the material for the next major assignment. This makes the task seem less daunting when you embark upon it.

As it is difficult to change your biological clock, it is wiser to capitalize on your most productive time.

Biorhythm theory

Another explanation of why our moods fluctuate from time to time and why our mental abilities increase and decrease and our physical energy waxes and wanes, lies in the theory of biorhythms. This is based on the belief that the body operates on three constantly recurring cycles. The first is a physical cycle that was discovered by Herman Swoboda, a psychologist at the University of Vienna in the latter half of the 19th century. He observed a 23-day cycle in the physical vitality of his patients, defined as strength, speed coordination, physiology and resistance to disease.

At about the same time, the work of a German physician, Wilhelm Fliess, led him to conclude that creativity, sensitivity, mental health and general moods fluctuate in 28-day cycles – the emotional cycle. Later an Austrian physician, Alfred Telcher, who was also a teacher at Innsbruck, advanced the view that memory, alertness, logical thinking and other analytical functions – the intellectual cycle – fluctuate on a 33-day pattern.

According to the biorhythm theory, the three cycles – physical, emotional and intellectual – start at birth, at a neutral baseline or zero point. From there each cycle rises in a positive phase during which the energies and abilities associated with the cycle are high. For the first half of its duration the cycle rises gradually to a peak, then goes into a decline. Each cycle fluctuates in an even and unending wave terminated only by death. Halfway through each cycle – 11.5 days in the physical cycle, 14 days in the emotional cycle and 16.5 days in the intellectual cycle – we enter a negative phase wherein all energies are recharged; hence capabilities are low or diminished. However, the weakest and most vulnerable days are not during the negative phase, when batteries are being recharged, but are when the cycle crosses the zero point or median line in either direction. During this limbo period – neither positive nor negative – a person is subject to mental lapses. And if two curves are crossing the median line on the same day, that is doubly unfortunate.

Owing to the different lengths of each cycle, it is likely on any given day that some rhythms are high and others low. Hence you

Table 7.1 Characteristics of the three biorhythm cycles

(0 signifies 'limbo' periods)

Cycle (length)	Energy level	Position in cycle (day nos.)	Period title	Characteristics
Physical (23 days)	+	2 to 14	peak days	endurance and strength high
	0	1 and 12	critical days	accident-prone – caution
	–	13 to 23	ebb days	reduce activity – rest
Emotional (28 days)	+	2 to 14	harmonious days	enjoy social relationships
	0	1 and 15	critical days	unstable – caution
	–	16 to 28	stress days	moodiness and negativity
Intellectual (33 days)	+	2 to 16	creative days	keen perception and judgement
	0	1 and 17	critical days	Error-prone – caution
	–	18 to 33	below-par days	avoid decisions or new projects

seldom have absolutely wonderful days or absolutely bad days as there is a majority of in-between days. Table 7.1 sets out the main characteristics of the days in all three cycles.

To determine your biorhythm, calculate the number of days since your birth and divide this figure by the length of each cycle. The result can then be plotted on a chart; a number of firms offer computer printouts for this. Alternatively, to facilitate quick and accurate calculations, Casio markets an electronic calculator called the Biolator.

According to one writer on the subject, Bernard Gittelson, business people who are familiar with the theory will not sign crucial contracts on emotionally or intellectually critical days.

What validity there is in the theory has not yet been satisfactorily resolved, although a vast number of studies have been made in attempts to prove or disprove it. For example, a Swiss behavioural scientist, Hans Schwing, found that 600 accidents he studied occurred on critical days, while Reinbold Bochon, a German scientist, charted 497 farm accidents and found that 98 per cent happened on critical days. Similarly, the Ohmi Railway Company in Japan – one of 5,000 Japanese companies to use biorhythm training to reduce accidents – the civic transport system in Zurich and the National Lead Company in America have all reported favourably on experiments designed to reduce or control accident rates by implementing biorhythm.

A self-fulfilling prophecy? Or simply evidence that warning the workers accounts for the indisputable drop in accidents? Or could it be evidence of the validity of biorhythm? If so, then what triggers these cycles at birth? And what determines their duration?

Circadian rhythm

Another school of thought argues that humans have lots of cycles. The most powerful are the circadian rhythms – the term means 'about a day' – denoting the regular ebb and flow in the body's internal chemistry. These rhythmic fluctuations in body chemistry and daily physiological processes are shown up by body temperature, metabolic and heart rates, urine flow and many other physiological functions.

The circadian rhythm is regarded as being 24 hours in duration. Humans, most animals and plants follow a 24-hour day by taking their cues from the earth's rotation. However, if people are isolated in underground caves for several weeks, circadian rhythms, including the sleep–wake cycle, start to drift. In a high proportion of people, and for reasons scientists cannot explain, they stabilize at around 25 hours. If this is the 'natural' length, researchers have concluded that people should control their lives by various time cues. These may be physical, eg sunrise to sunset, or social, eg mechanical clock time and meal times.

It is argued that mechanical clock time leads people to go to bed an hour earlier each day than their body clocks would prefer. At weekends, when some cues are weakened, people are more likely to follow the body clock by going to bed an hour later than usual on Friday night and two hours later on Saturday. On Sunday they return to the conventional cycle for workday demands and on 'blue Monday', not surprisingly, they may feel less alert.

Jet lag and other irregular effects

The natural rhythm or normal routine of the body is altered when factors such as air travel, with its rapid crossing of time zones, or the introduction of official Summer Time intrude. When this happens, temporary difficulty occurs in readjusting the body rhythms. In turn, this affects the sleep cycle, the endocrine glands and body temperature. The temporary imbalance that results can lead to fatigue, loss of concentration and efficiency and possibly accidents. This effect is far more pronounced when travel occurs on an east–west axis.

There are other factors apart from international flying that can have uncomfortable effects on the body's natural rhythm. Shift work is one of these, and is normally patterned in one of the following ways:

permanent unsocial hours; these particularly affect night security officers, office cleaners, medical professionals, police officers and military personnel;

short permanent or slowly rotating shifts, eg one or two weeks at a time on a particular shift, followed by rotation to a different shift;

continual or rapidly rotating shifts, ie the same shift is never worked more than twice in succession.

From the evidence available, it appears that the rapidly rotating system is one of the best suited to persons working on complex tasks. This is because the tasks are best done when the workers' rhythms have not yet settled down to the slower pace of night work, as happens on permanent or slowly rotating shifts.

Research indicates that, in general, performance is at its best when the body is most active and the body temperature is at its highest. Considerably more research needs to be done by chronobiologists and others to provide a better match between the body's capability level and the tasks to be done. The growth of shift working on nuclear reactors and computer installations gives increased urgency to this because of the potential scale of the consequences should a major error occur. For example, the famous accident at Three Mile Island occurred at 4 am, which happens to be the time at which most people are at their circadian low point for energy and efficiency. Furthermore, the workers concerned had been changing shifts every week.

To some degree, people can train themselves to cope with un-social hours. For example:

if possible, structure your job in such a manner that you can take short breaks and do some exercises;
eat healthy foods;
keep a diary of your drowsiness, and avoid doing very important or boring tasks during this period.

However, in the final analysis we are all very different in the way in which our body-temperature curves vary throughout any time period and we need to be aware of our own particular characteristics. Only then can we be sure that our prime time is being used to our best advantage and that we are truly matching our tasks to our capability level.

In conclusion, to parody Ecclesiastes (with apologies to Solomon):

For every manager there is a season
And a time for every matter under heaven;

A time for employees and a time for the boss;
A time for some planning, or else the day's lost;
A time to read mail, and a time to discard;
A time for 'time off' when the stress is too hard;
A time for a crisis, with adequate breaks;
A time to achieve, and a time for mistakes;
A time for committees (if agenda they'll trim);
A time to be 'out' and a time to be 'in';
A time to take phone calls, and a time to ignore;
A time to retreat, then reopen your door;
A time to decide and a time to delay;
A time to ensure that your staff have their say;
A time for your doing, and a time for delegation;
A time for quick thinking, or for deep rumination;
A time to say 'yes' and a time to say 'no';
A time to come early, and to know when to go;
A time to give praise for the work that you see;
And time to reserve for your own family.

08

Analysing and improving your time expenditure

I never waste a single moment at the office – I'm hard at it from the moment I get in until long after everybody else has gone home.

Stressed-out manager

Many people tend to be victims of their own habit patterns in the way they use their working day, without having a clear idea of how their time is spent. Some have never consciously brought the problem to mind; others make guesses, which can be wildly inaccurate, based on their preconceived ideas or good intentions.

If a manager claims, 'Yesterday I spent two-thirds of my time with customers,' fully believing that they did so, it is more than likely that their actual customer contact was less than a third of the working day; the remainder was more likely to have been taken up with travelling, internal meetings, handling paperwork, checking e-mails and the like.

A surprising amount of time that we think we are using productively is lost without our realizing it. Nearly all of us have unconscious habits that lead to our time being stolen from us.

Some potential time stealers

Check if you suffer from any of these:

- innumerable e-mails;
- telephone interruptions;
- the 'My door is always open' approach;
- excessive socializing;
- drop-in visitors;
- visitors who will not leave;

- other people rambling on in discussions at meetings or losing the point of the subject under discussion;
- colleagues making mistakes that you need to correct;
- failure to delegate and taking on too much;
- losing control;
- fear of small errors and as a consequence verifying excessively;
- addiction to detailed data;
- difficulty in making unpleasant or awkward decisions;
- irrational decision-making methods;
- failure to implement decisions;
- excessive reading.

If you are seriously intent on becoming a better time manager, it is important to get the record straight as to what you are spending your time on at present. Without an accurate baseline, you will have no reference point for assessing your scope for improvements or for evaluating the savings resulting from those improvements.

Remember: once objectives have been agreed, then it is organization, organization, organization.

Keeping a time log

There is only one satisfactory solution: keep a simple time log for a sample period, such as that shown in Table 8.1. You may protest that such an exercise will in itself be a waste of your time but be assured that this time will be well repaid in greater effectiveness later. By recording your use of time in detail, you may unearth problems and practices of which you were previously totally unaware.

In constructing your log, select a representative period, one that is as typical as possible of the average condition throughout your year, avoiding any seasonal peaks or troughs. The best duration for such a study will vary from one manager to another but an initial sample of one typical week should be sufficient. In any event, you should repeat the study at intervals to squeeze out any inefficiencies that may creep back in.

Table 8.1 Specimen time log for part of a day

Date: Tuesday Jan 15				Sheet 1
From	To	Activity	Value to me*	Comments
8.30	9.00	Reading mail	M	Shapes the day
9.00	9.15	Replying to e-mails	M	
9.15	9.35	Instructing direct report	H	Minimizing interruptions
9.35	9.45	Working on xyz report	H	Major planned task
9.45	10.00	Phone call from boss	L	Querying yesterday's figures
10.00	10.05	Phoned area office	L	Dealing with boss's query
10.05	10.10	More work on report	H	Completed stage 3
10.10	10.30	Coffee and toilet	M	

*H = high, M = medium, L = low

Most people will have to do their own recording, possibly assisted, guided or bullied by their direct report or some intelligent and interested junior. If you spend the majority of your time in the presence of these direct reports, you may even be able to delegate the whole recording job to them.

Here are some guidelines for drawing up a daily time log:

- Keep it simple, in a form that is easy for you to handle.
- Make sure it is always to hand.
- Record activities as they occur; alternatively, update every 15 minutes during quiet periods. Activities cannot accurately be logged from memory later in the day.
- Keep the entries short but sufficiently specific; excessive detail can be counterproductive.
- Record all interruptions, however small.
- Subdivide long uninterrupted periods spent on an extended task into its various stages. It is unnecessary to account for every single minute and it will not affect the analysis if the record is a few minutes out at the end of the day.
- At the end of the sample period, analyse into your chosen categories how much time was spent on each. Do this daily, weekly and over the whole period of study. If the various categories are each given a separate file card, the analysis can be simplified by collating onto its card all the observations

relating to a particular category, thereby saving unnecessary paperwork.

One approach is the individual four-by-six-inch card on which you can make all entries for a single recorded incident. At the end of the day, collate all the cards. This system may be more convenient than completing a larger composite form, particularly if you are absent from the office for extended periods. A second advantage is that collating the material can be done in any sequence or combination required. Alternatively, you can use a computer schedule if it is more convenient.

A variation is to concentrate on one item at a time. For example, you may be concerned about the number of interruptions that occur. With each interruption make a note on a suitably pre-printed card. Immediately after the interruption, jot down the name of the person, duration, time and cause. Entries should be specific but short. On analysis at the end of the day, you can give some thought, if necessary, to devising suitable strategies to secure more effective use of time.

Whichever system you use, avoid the following pitfalls:

- trusting to memory by leaving entries to a 'more convenient time'; our memories do not serve us well in such circumstances;
- omitting significant details such as whether a diversion was self-imposed or externally inflicted;
- self-deception in the interests of personal face-saving. When, for instance does the entry 'creative thinking' become a cover for daydreaming or fantasizing?

After keeping a time log identifying your time wasters and arriving at solutions to deal with them:

implement these solutions;
check your progress;
make a new time log.

For example, did you ever think of the number of interruptions you have every day? Did you ever wonder how many of these are unnecessary? Business people appear to assume the automatic legitimacy of each interruption. But how many interruptions do the following professionals have while conducting their work:

a surgeon in an operating theatre?
a professor giving a lecture?
a marriage counsellor during a session with a troubled couple?
a clergyman or -woman during a service?
an airline pilot during a flight?

Job analysis

After completing the analysis of your sample period, it is good practice to examine your data in the light of some clear ideas about what your job actually involves: ie how your time should be apportioned overall. If you have a boss, their ideas on this may well differ from your own. To overcome this possibility, both you and your boss should independently complete a job analysis worksheet in respect of *your* job. This involves each of you assessing the percentage of your total time that is meant to be spent on the various major activity areas the job comprises and then ranking these percentages in two ways:

in order of the amount of time devoted to each activity area;
in order of the value or contribution of each activity area to the overall goals of the organization. This is a subjective assessment by both of you.

An example of such a worksheet is given in Table 8.2.

Efficiency, effectiveness and excellence

It is important at this time to understand the distinction between efficiency and effectiveness. Efficiency means doing things right, or operating as economically as possible; effectiveness means doing the right things, or making sure that your time is spent on those activities that produce the most positive benefits in terms of the goals towards which you are working. Excellence is efficiency X effectiveness, namely *doing the right things right*.

Table 8.2 Job analysis worksheet

Activities, tasks or projects	% time spent per week	Ranking	
		By time	By value
Customer contact	25	2	1
Staff relations	20	3	3
Statistical returns	10	4=	4
Technical problem solving	35	1	2
Monthly report	10	4=	5

Obviously, this is what the job analysis is concerned with. Nobody wins medals for performing an operation more cheaply if it is something that should never be done at all, eg designing a more efficient filing system for obsolete correspondence. What you are after is a method of spending your time in a way that will make a bigger contribution to the objectives of your organization through the objectives of your job. This means eliminating as far as possible all those non-essential and low-return activities that consume your time.

To do this you could start by going back over the analysis of the first sample period you used for your time log, making a further classification of each entry into 'productive' and 'non-productive' in terms of your job objectives. A productive activity may be defined as anything that contributes to or accomplishes a work function or goal related to personal or unit objectives, eg a meeting that resulted in key decisions affecting your unit or department. A non-productive activity makes no such contribution, eg a meeting with little or no direction and which resulted in prolonged discussion and boredom. Table 8.3 gives an abbreviated example of this form of analysis.

The number of boxes and types of activity will be determined by the nature of your job, so include only those that are relevant to your particular range of activities.

Within each box, state briefly your 'label' for the particular piece of work you were doing and designate it P (productive) or NP (non-productive), depending on whether or not you feel the time was productively spent.

Table 8.3 Personal time analysis form

Date:						
Sheet no:						
When *(15-minute* *slots)*	*Activity*	*Where*			*Initiator*	
		own office	*elsewhere*		*self*	*other: name*
	Meetings, personal contacts, planning. Inspecting, instructing, paperwork, personal breaks, telephone (in/out). Other headings as appropriate, one column for each.					

At the end of each day or sample period, you can begin your analysis by expressing the total of each column as a percentage of the total time spent. These percentages can be aggregated over several periods to give an overall pattern with day-to-day variations. Compare the results of your analysis with your prior guesses of how you expected your time to be apportioned.

When you have totalled each column over a week or two, you will probably be surprised at how much of your time was non-productive in these terms, even though you may feel that you were generally working at full stretch. Remember, effective time management is measured by output (results) and not input (effort). Effectiveness is the product of what a manager achieves, not of how busy they are. Perspiration, or work rate, is no substitute for results.

The cost of your non-productive time may also come as a shock to you. The price or cost of a commodity often dramatizes the difference in attitude between giving away what is free and making judicious use of a precious resource that is expensive and irreplaceable. Refer back to Table 2.1 in Chapter 2 to aid your assessment of this distinction.

The final proof of whether or not you have really effected the improvements you seek will necessitate keeping another log for a further sample period; thus you can measure your revised allocation of time and compare it with the first period.

Work logs

Alternatively, you can prepare a basic work log supported by a series of subsidiary logs, such as a telephone log or a visitor log. For example, interruptions may be categorized by:

> number;
> when;
> type, eg visitors, telephone, self, if you yield to a sudden impulse to do something else;
> reason why activity was terminated, eg work completed, change by self, change by others.

It may be advisable to analyse down to foreseen or unforeseen interruptions. The former include situations where a direct report is told, 'Let me see it as soon as it is completed.'

When most of the entries are shown as terminated, this is a good indicator that personal planning is effective; while if there is a high reading on activities changed by you yourself, this may be an indication that you are too easily diverted and switch from high- to low-priority tasks, or that inadequate time is being allowed.

Work sampling

An alternative and more sophisticated form of time measurement is the work-sampling approach. This technique is based on probability theory, which enables you to generalize to a total situation from snap observations made of your activities. This is similar to taking opinion polls from a random or balanced sample of the public. To use this method correctly means giving prior thought to how you select the sample of snap observations without biasing the result; probably someone else should do it for you. But it can be done and you can learn a lot from the results if you are willing to accept them as truthful.

An alternative is a desktop device capable of recording your activities up to 30 times a day. At the sound of randomly spaced bleeps a note or snapshot is made of what is happening at that moment.

Follow-up action

Once you have analysed how you spend your time – and many of us are surprised by our fragmented working pattern – you can:

identify things that need not be done;
identify activities that can be done just as well by someone else;
identify the time wasters;
check that daily goals contribute to long-range goals.

The analysis may also reveal a pattern indicating which parts of your day are the most productive. In turn, this may stimulate you to analyse how the less productive parts of the day can be made more productive.

You can undertake further analysis regarding the sources of work:

Your boss: are they using you as a direct report?
Direct reports: have they been allowed to become too dependent on you?
Self: are you taking on too many tasks?
Others: why are you receiving work from them, and how important is it?

Initially this does take time but the pay-off will justify the effort many times over.

09

Organizing your workload

I feel like a beast of burden. I don't know how I'll ever get through this load of work. Everybody seems to want everything done at once, or preferably yesterday.

Anonymous

After analysing how your time is spent, it may be desirable to analyse your time problems into personal and external.

Personal category problems

These may include:

psychological problems:
- inability to say no;
- lack of self-discipline;
- perfectionism;
- procrastination.

organizational problems:
- failure to distinguish between the important few and the trivial many;
- inability to complete one job at a time.

relationship problems:
- failure to delegate;
- failure to control aggressiveness.

External category problems

These may include:

things relating to the person:
- too many interruptions;
- too many meetings.

organizational problems:
- – excessive bureaucracy;
- – excessive paperwork.

The following sections show ways to deal with these and other time-related problems.

Effective personal organization

Many management jobs, contrary to much popular belief, are characterized by a highly fragmented work pattern. Managers rarely concentrate on one job for any sustained period of time. However, such fragmentation is more a reflection of the manager's style than the demands of the job. Managers tend to be the victims of their own habits. In practice, breaking such habits can be very difficult and requires the exercise of self-discipline. Ways have to be devised to reinforce new and better behaviour patterns.

Goals, as identified from the completion of the job analysis worksheet, should be examined. Goal clarification enables a person to avoid confusing activity with results: in turn this can stop them from making long-term changes because of short-term pressures and allowing the urgent to drive out the important. To establish goals we need:

- Long-term goals – spanning the next five years or longer. These need to be reviewed periodically to determine if they have changed.
- Medium-term goals – spanning the next six months.
- Short-term goals – planned on a weekly basis.
- Daily goals, for which planning must be done either before starting the working day or at the end of the preceding day.

Use of planning guides

Many different sorts of planning guides are available commercially. You can also design your own to meet any special requirements. These include calendars, wall charts, desk diaries and software (eg MS Outlook) to help you keep track of important dates and meetings and to plan your year ahead as a whole or month by month. Similarly, monthly and weekly planning guides exist that enable more detailed scheduling. Possible items for inclusion in these are:

- scheduled activities: luncheons, meeting times, deadlines for reports;
- key projects: progress checks, required changes, priority tasks;
- staff matters: meetings with individuals, priority work areas.

You may also design your own planning aid, such as an electronic diary. This operates by a desktop computer or laptop recording in its memory all your appointments, so that recall of appointments onto a screen can be presented under one of several headings: name of appointee, date, time of day, nature of appointment, etc. This enables you to analyse the structure of your activities, since you can ask your diary to list all your appointments relating to a particular type of work, category of appointee, etc, and thus identify the areas that absorb most of your time.

Finally, daily planners are available that go into more detail than is possible in your desk diary, and that enable you to plan your time for particularly critical days in the near future. An example is given in Table 9.1. Note that although this shows fixed times, it does not tackle the question of priorities.

Daily 'Do' list

The 'Do' list is a variation of the daily planning chart, but instead of concentrating on specific times it begins by setting priorities in those parts of the day that are not already pre-scheduled. It is one of the most effective methods for improving your personal time management because you:

Table 9.1 Daily organizer and action plan

Day and date ....

	Fixed-time tasks or appointments	*Essential tasks that must be done today*
pre 9.00		1
9.00		2
9.30		3
10.00		4
10.30		5
11.00		
11.30		People to see
Noon		
12.30		
1.00		
1.30		People to e-mail or telephone
2.00		
2.30		
3.00		Paperwork to complete
3.30		
4.00		
4.30		Tasks carried forward from today – to follow up or remember
5.00		
5.30		
6.00		
post 6.00		

- keep sight of your objectives;
- focus on the important and urgent;
- concentrate on one task at a time;
- avoid wasting time on the trivial and unimportant;
- are more likely to delegate all that can be delegated.

The list can be compiled at the start of each day or preferably at the end of the previous day's work. You start by writing down on a sheet of paper a complete list of the unfinished tasks that are currently on your mind or need to be tackled within your next time frame. Calling it a 'Do' list rather than a 'To do' list makes it more emphatic.

In preparing the 'Do' list, points to note include:

- Be proactive, not reactive.
- Be demanding of yourself but realistic, and budget for only about three-quarters of your time. People tend to be over-optimistic.
- Learn to estimate the time required for each job. To accomplish what you plan to do requires that you are able to estimate the time required for each task. It is frustrating to take two hours over a job for which you budgeted 30 minutes. Further, when discrepancies arise, consider how you can reduce the time needed when you are next confronted with the task. Initially, an aid to achieving this is to complete a form along the lines of Table 9.2.
- Remember that tasks can change priority as circumstances change, eg at your boss's request or with the passage of time. In the latter case, dealing with a tax problem may be a C job on Monday, but it may well become an A by Thursday.
- If a task keeps getting postponed, you need to ask yourself whether this is because of its time priority being low or whether it is evidence of your procrastination.
- The list should always be kept available and in the same place, and preferably on your person so that it is to hand even when you are not at your workstation. Likewise, keep a small diary or notebook rather than odd scraps of paper for recording

ideas that occur to you when away from your own office or use your laptop.

■ Ask yourself what you want to get from each activity on your list, and how you want to behave in particular situations, eg direct and formal or patient and responsive.

Setting priorities

The next step consists of sorting your tasks into three priority categories:

A: those you *must* do;
B: those you *should* do if possible;
C: those you *could* do if you find yourself with some time to spare.

The As, of which there should not be too many, are then graded A1, A2, A3, etc in order of their importance; likewise Bs and Cs. In this way your order of tackling them can be related to their importance and urgency, reducing in advance any confusion between your activities and your results.

But take care not to grade things A simply because they are what you enjoy doing. Likewise, do things because they are necessary and not because they are nice.

In assessing the significance and priority of these tasks, it is a good idea to involve your direct report, if you have one, so that any relevant papers you will need can be produced and codified before they reach your desk. Having established these priorities, each task should then be entered in the intended order of tackling on a sheet similar to the one in Table 9.2.

As far as possible, pay regard to your preferred work style. For example, some people prefer to break up their working days and schedule brief spells of concentrated work between appointments. Other people are focused and do one thing at a time. Still others are stimulated by tackling several things at once.

Whenever possible, group similar jobs and try to deal with several jobs from the same group in a particular time slot.

Table 9.2 Prioritized 'Do' list

Priority task list for today: date . . . .

Priority	Task	Deadline	Estimated duration	Fixed time[1]	Time taken
A1					
A2					
A3					
B1					
B2					
B3					
B4					
C1					
C2					

Scheduled meetings, visitors, telephone calls to, etc to be allowed for:

Scheduled time	Item	Duration	
		planned	actual

1. Fixed time refers to tasks which are related to such things as the availability of, say, some equipment or to banking hours and can only be done at certain times.
2. It may not be enough to say 'Call X.' You may need to add the phone number and reason for calling. It may also be appropriate to have coded symbols to record progress, eg na: no answer; wcb: will call back.

Keep visible all key tasks on your schedule for the day. This will increase the certainty of dealing with them – you cannot do what has slipped from your memory. That's why it's important to have both an electronic copy and a hard copy.

Follow-up

Periodically you should address the following questions:

Were the goals demanding yet realistic?
Did setting daily goals result in increased effectiveness, and if not, why not?
Which period of the day was most productive, and why?
Which period was least productive, and why?
Is this a normal work pattern?
What was the longest period of uninterrupted working time? (After listing causes of interruptions, indicate action to be taken to control them.)
Who/what was the most frequent cause of interruption?
What could have been delegated or not done at all?

The preparation of a 'Do today' list can go a long way towards ensuring effective use of your time. However, you should not plan for every moment of the day; the unexpected may happen. Effective managers learn to respond to such interruptions.

As part of this exercise, try to anticipate; this is generally more effective than remedial action. Also, identify key result areas. Remember the Pareto principle from Chapter 5, which tells us that 20 per cent of our effort can result in 80 per cent of our achievements.

For most people these can be the key result areas; they are the proactive tasks that we are really employed to do, as opposed to the purely reactive ones on the previous list. However, it is all too easy to forget the prime objective of draining the swamp when you are up to the waist in alligators!

There is a low pay-off from time spent on activities such as routine tasks and day-to-day activities. In contrast, there may be a high pay-off from time spent on planning, delegating, developing personnel and thinking creatively. These are items that are important but not urgent.

Urgency versus importance

As part of the exercise of classifying and scheduling your tasks, it is important to be able to distinguish between their importance and their urgency – two concepts that are often confused. The importance of a task is determined by how closely it relates to the key results that are directly related to your job purpose or objective. The urgency of a task is determined by how soon it needs to be completed. Urgency increases as a deadline approaches.

In reality these two concepts are independent of each other and can be separately assessed. Tasks may be plotted on a grid as in Figure 9.1 to help determine your priorities for the day.

The tyranny of the urgent

In practice what often happens is:

Important and urgent. Because these jobs are urgent and therefore may be done too hurriedly, often they don't get done very well. Rushing a job can lead to serious adverse results.

Important but not urgent. Although these jobs are vital, they may get overlooked and not be done at all because they are not urgent; more immediate considerations cause them to be repeatedly postponed.

Not important but urgent. Simply because of their urgency, too much attention is given to these ephemeral jobs, which have no long-term importance. This category often contains the most serious time wasters. People succumb to the tyranny of the urgent, allowing it to drive out the more important tasks.

Neither important nor urgent. It is doubtful whether these tasks should ever have been accepted in the first place. An example is an invitation to address a luncheon club, which a busy manager could have declined or delegated when it was suggested more than a month ago. Because it was then neither important nor urgent, it was probably given no attention. But it has now become urgent because the lunch is tomorrow and the speech has not yet been prepared. The passage of time has made it more urgent, though it remains unimportant; so it has to be prepared today.

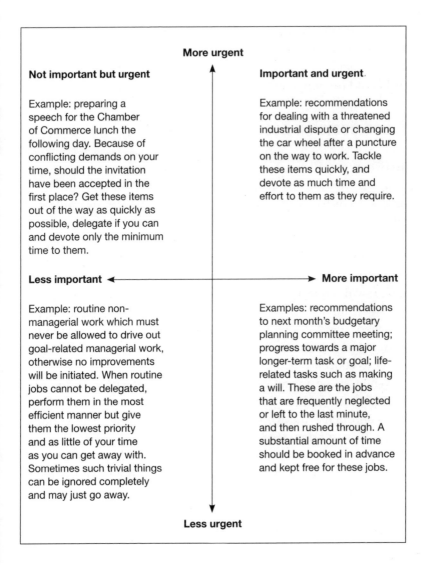

Figure 9.1 Urgency versus importance

Although urgency can increase with time, or decrease on rare occasions when a deadline is relaxed, importance normally remains unchanged except in rare circumstances where there is a change in the effects or results required from the job. If a major project on which you have been working is cancelled through loss of an order or lack of funds, its importance disappears. To distinguish between the important and the urgent, ask yourself, 'If I could do only one thing today, what would it be?'

A bad decision because of urgency

To overcome the tyranny of the urgent, it is important to learn to make the right decision about what to do in an emergency and to assess correctly degrees of importance. Here is an example of a situation where this requirement was not handled well.

The financial manager of a company needed urgent repairs to a damaged safe door. When he approached the maintenance department he was informed that no fitters were available for the next few days, as they were engaged on the task of fitting special catches to all the windows in the building. By having these catches attached, windows would be prevented from being opened too wide. Meanwhile, all other maintenance work had been halted in order to concentrate on the window job.

When asked for an explanation, a shamefaced colleague revealed that a sudden gust of wind earlier in the day had blown back an open window, tearing it from its fittings. The window had fallen and damaged the roof of the chairman's car. This was obviously important to the chairman but how important was it, relatively speaking, to the company as a whole? The damage to the car had already occurred, so urgency no longer existed, whereas the insecure safe door had become an immediate and serious hazard requiring top-priority action.

Working through your 'Do' list

When embarking on your list of tasks, try to devote your total attention to one task at a time and to complete it correctly the first time. If you cannot devote the time to doing it right the first time, when will you have time? Don't make the mistake of pre-planning for every moment of the day, but allow for the fact that the unexpected may happen. In everybody's job, more in some cases than others, there is always an element of work that involves reacting to the needs and demands of others who are pursuing their own job objectives; so plan some reactive time into each day and train others to approach you at the time you have set aside for this purpose. Effective managers learn to anticipate and handle the unexpected with the same efficiency with which they tackle their regular work, which is generally better than having to take remedial action afterwards because contingencies were not foreseen. Remember the old saying: if anything can go wrong, it probably will!

Also, reserve some time for thinking; if you cannot find this time in the normal course of events it is quite legitimate to make an appointment in your diary with yourself just as you would with any other person. Let your direct report know that this is your time set aside for thinking, to ensure you are free from interruptions.

At the end of the day

Although there will be some unexpected interruptions during the day, there will come a point when you will have to accept the inevitable and bring your working day to a close. As far as any uncompleted tasks are concerned, try to make the break at a point that facilitates an effective restart later. This can best be achieved in one of the following ways:

- ending at some natural point of intermediate accomplishment, eg when some sub-goal has been reached;
- putting the work into a physical shape that will enable a prompt and easy restart;
- clarifying the nature of the problem or hindrance if the work is temporarily set aside at a point of frustration; this will leave the problem in your subconscious mind, which will continue working on it until you are again able to give it your full attention.

The fact that you have prepared your 'Do' list has gone a long way towards ensuring the best possible use of your time, and there will be another list tomorrow. So don't feel too unhappy if not every task on the list has been finished by the end of the day, as long as you have worked in accordance with your priorities. It may simply indicate that you have been attempting too much. Bring forward your important unfinished tasks for inclusion in tomorrow's list and you will gradually become more adept at adjusting your expectations to fit the time available.

Some jobs are too big to complete in one day; when preparing a major report it may be necessary to break it down into significant segments – eg writing the introduction, preparing the section on costings – and making an early start on these. Too large a task may be daunting, so breaking it down will overcome troublesome psychological barriers. Refer back to the 'Swiss cheese' approach mentioned in Chapter 5: make some significant holes in the job at the first opportunity and expand on these so that eventually they join up, and much of the substance will by then have been digested. You can pursue this idea and make better use of those few free minutes just before lunch by collating some of the data required for your jumbo report.

Time not used in this manner can very easily be wasted altogether or misused on some relatively unimportant C job.

Finally, remember that it is much more productive to look back with satisfaction on what has been achieved than to berate yourself for the things that still remain to be done.

10

Organizing your workplace

The Pentagon – that immense monument to modern man's subservience to the desk.

Lord Oliver Franks

Franks's comments need not have the same relevance today, for information and communication technology are changing the geography of work, and the need for office space is shrinking. For an increasing number of people, work no longer happens at a central workplace. Instead of going to the office, the office comes to them via the internet. People may work at home, at a mobile office if they are on the road for extended periods of time, or they may use hot-desking and similar arrangements. The need for office space is further reduced because the use of computers means that less filing space is required. Individuals balance work and home commitments. In turn, organizations gain from a more flexible workplace. But it can lead to isolated workers.

For some the office will become a place for the social aspects of work – networking, lunching, gossiping – while the real work will be done by telecommunication.

Within offices there is a shift away from the 'hive' type of office – the departmentalized office structure – to the 'den', 'cell' and 'club', where teams of people organize themselves and their space around functions and projects. Today there is a lot more interaction across the old barriers. Further, recent analyses of traffic patterns in the office show that a reconfiguration of the space to funnel traffic through common areas where people would naturally mingle boosts interaction tenfold.

Meanwhile, however successful you may be at prioritizing your work, it is unlikely that you will be a good time manager if your office, whatever style it may take, is always in a mess. Organizing the workplace is often a personal matter that depends on taste and working habits in addition to the task requirement.

Some factors to bear in mind in the traditional office are shown below.

Location

In selecting the location of the office, consideration should be given to its functions. Is it a:

- meeting place?
- postbox?
- filing centre?
- working place?

If time is spent working at home, ask why. It may be:

- because quiet time is required;
- from force of habit;
- from preference;
- from necessity.

Space

Offices may be divided into two areas:

> **Pressure:** the zone around the desk. This is a setting for formal conversation in which the usual occupant of the chair behind the desk takes the lead. A desk serves as a barrier, hence it is best to sit behind it if a reprimand has to be given. A round table suggests positive progressive discipline, while an oblong table with someone sitting at the head suggests punitive discipline.
> **Semi-social:** the zone away from the desk, in which there may be armchairs and a coffee table.

In determining the floor space, regard should be paid to both personal space and adequate work space.

Research in proxemics reveals that there are basic distances of interaction. When violations occur, increased tension and distrust can ensue. Accordingly, office furniture should be organized to ensure personal space.

Linked to this is the question of privacy. This takes on quite different meanings depending on whether you occupy a closed-door office or an open-space area with or without partitions. In the former you are automatically assured of a significant amount of privacy, whereas in a completely open area you must develop subtler means to achieve this. You need to determine the actual boundaries of your workplace, then try to arrange your furniture. Plants or personal articles can act as a visual indication of your area. Some companies provide quiet rooms or desks where staff can work when they need to be undisturbed.

Proper consideration should also be given to how a direct report shares the use of space, even though they may have a separate room.

If much travel is involved, ideally there should be a place to change clothes and store items of luggage.

Occupancy time

If the proportion of occupancy time is low, is there adequate time for:

information sharing, thinking and planning?
seeing people, particularly those requiring advice and mentoring?

If the proportion of occupancy time is high, are you:

too readily available?
in a rut?
seeing persons in the right place?
aware of what is happening in your unit?

Getting rid of the desk may break the chain that binds you to the office.

Equipment

The requisite equipment should be available, with easy access to the tools most frequently used. A wise rule is: a place for everything and everything in its place.

When the function of an office includes meetings, it is preferable to have a separate table to sit around rather than the desk. A small coffee table may also be useful, where there is work on a one-to-one basis, as a means of establishing a more friendly atmosphere between the interactors.

Where space is limited because of high cost, perhaps a mini-office should be purchased. A table-desk will give a less crowded feeling than a cube desk of the same dimensions, and wood of a light colour will help reduce its apparent size.

Is your desk really necessary?

In many offices desks are unnecessary; they are a barrier to communication and may be incorrectly used. Many people have them because they require a surface on which to write or use their computer. Alternatively, you could opt for a small writing table.

Where a desk is needed, some people favour facing a wall while working to ensure minimum distraction. Further, when seeing someone it is necessary to turn away from the desk, thereby ensuring that full attention is paid to visitors. Alternatively, there may be a work table behind the desk, which can offer a degree of privacy. A swivel chair allows you to switch between tasks both physically and psychologically.

Desk-level lighting may be preferred to overhead lighting because it is more concentrated. But, whenever possible, daylight is the best form of illumination, as it is more humanizing.

The writing surface should be comfortable for use. As a rule, glass tops and highly polished surfaces should be avoided because the glare they give off can cause eye strain. Many tasks are made easier by a slight slope in the writing surface.

Many desks are too wide. Work is not necessarily expedited by having a large desk; indeed, with more surface area, good housekeeping may suffer. Clutter may be allowed to expand to fill the space available. In turn, clutter can create a feeling of being overwhelmed. Only paper relating to the current job should be there. Failure to maintain this discipline makes it easy to become sidetracked by tasks that may be more appealing or interesting. Remember the wise proverb: a tidy desk is the sign of a tidy mind.

Where additional workspace is periodically required, an L-shaped extension to the desk can be provided.

Personal effects – eg photographs and souvenirs – should not be on the desk; they can be put on a shelf or side table. This avoids distraction and loss of working space.

Desk drawers are a mixed blessing. Too many people use them as temporary stores and sometimes important papers may get lost in them. Use them with care.

Reorganize your desk periodically. Here is one possible procedure for doing this:

1 If you are not yet working towards a paperless office, get a large waste bin.
2 Take everything off the top of the desk and empty all drawers.
3 Discard items no longer of any use.
4 Take each of the remaining items and put them on trial for their life.
5 Ask of each in turn, 'What will happen if this is thrown away?'
6 You will find that a large proportion of the items will be expendable.
7 Put only the retained items back in the desk.
8 Review all desk files to ensure they are active.

Miscellaneous pieces of paper that do not fit into an existing active file can be real desk clutterers. These can be handled by opening three special files labelled:

ideas: for notes written by yourself;
self-development: for course brochures and other things relating to your personal learning;
someday: for papers you may want one day and are reluctant to part with.

All these should of course be reviewed at appropriate intervals. Make a diary note now to do so on fixed future dates.

Due regard should also be paid to hot-desking and just-in-time desks. In getting rid of desks, substantial financial savings may result, for people are far less efficient at using office space than machines. A machine can work for 168 hours a week, while a person rarely uses a desk beyond 60 hours.

The cybercafé workplace

A growing number of organizations have introduced cybercafé workplaces. An internet-style café, at which beverages and food are available, can facilitate or ease new-style working. Such places equipped with PCs and laptop docking, all connected to the internet, can cater for the needs of mobile employees and those hot-desking. For example, they offer a convenient place for clients and employees, particularly those not working from 9 am to 5 pm, to meet or wait between meetings. Others who are working in open-plan offices and finding concentration difficult can also escape and work in the internet café.

Handling incoming papers and reports

Aim to handle each incoming piece of paper once only and keep it on the move. A pencil dot in the corner each time you handle it is a useful test of your success in this respect. But each time you pick up a piece of paper, make a decision about it. Basically you have only five options:

> bin it;
> refer it to someone else;
> act on it;
> shred it;
> file it.

With the second option you refer it to someone else not to get the monkey off your back (see Chapters 17 and 18) but because the other person is better able to handle the matter than you. Further, if you really want them to handle it, indicate on the item when you would like it back, and make a note in your calendar.

With the third option, when you do act on it, you should give total attention to the task so that it is completed correctly.

Keep non-urgent reports off your desk until you intend to read them. In addition, if you find that there are some that turn up regularly but never get read, arrange for your name to be removed from the distribution list and do not read any unless they are necessary and relevant to your job. Do the same for electronic reports.

When reports are being submitted to you by your junior staff, ensure that they arrive at reasonably spaced intervals and that they are not carrying an unwarranted level of detailed information. Also ensure that they are action-oriented and do not pose problems for your attention unless accompanied by alternative solutions with recommendations.

Your aim should be to clear your desk daily. In part this may be for reasons of security but there is the additional factor that a fresh start in the morning is psychologically desirable.

However, desks should not be cleared by slipping the contents into a drawer.

'Bring forward' file and message systems

It is essential that you have a method of automatically bringing things to your attention on specified dates. A calendar pad is helpful, but often an accordion file with a pocket for each day of the current month and pockets for subsequent months is the best method. Where a lot of paperwork has to be handled, a more elaborate system is necessary. If you prefer, this can be done electronically. You can check your computer each morning and those items will appear on the screen.

Not too many writing pads should be used. In many cases there can be dual-purpose pads, eg a routing slip and a telephone message pad may be combined. Each slip can have a telephone message blank on one side and a routing slip on the other, simply use the side needed at each particular moment.

Find a suitable chair

You should have a healthy chair – one that is firm and gives good back support. The weight should be on the bottom of the thighs and not on the base of the spine, while the height is usually correct when the weight of the knees is supported by the feet. This prevents pressure on the under part of the upper leg at the front edge of the seat.

With correct posture, seating fatigue is reduced, and this helps increase productivity and efficiency. Chairs with built-in hydraulic height-control handles are available. Furthermore, some chairs have a pop-up footrest for reclining or for a short power nap after lunch, and a built-in massager for backs.

The effects of colour

Colour can enhance performance at work or at home by creating a positive and satisfying atmosphere. Some psychological effects of the main colours are:

Red over-stimulates and increases blood pressure.
Black and brown create feelings of fatigue.
White produces no strong reactions but increases perception of light and space.

Blue is relaxing and helps lower blood pressure.
Yellow can cause eye strain if too bright, but is generally perceived as warm and creating a cheerful mood.
Green is the most normal and popular colour, consonant with nature. It can be perceived as physically cool.

When selecting colours for the purpose of workplace decoration, you should take the following factors into account:

What work functions will take place in the area? A formal conference room and reception area require a more dignified atmosphere than the staff room.
Where is the area located in relation to the remainder of the building? A well-lit sunny southern exposure requires a more restrained colour choice than a dim north-facing room.
What effect do you want to achieve?

Colour can enhance or reduce the mood and productivity of employees. Light and mid-range colours are more acceptable to the majority of people, and intense tones should usually be avoided. Similarly, the busier the pattern on wall coverings and curtains, the greater their impact and the more difficult it is to tolerate them for long periods. This can become an irritant and therefore a barrier to productivity.

Time-saving tips for homeworkers

When people work from home, the balance between work and personal life changes. Unless there is a clear contract delineating the roles and responsibilities of each partner, misunderstanding and possibly conflict can occur. Here are some guidelines to prevent this:

Arrange and equip separate office space.
Do not skimp on the PC, monitor and printer; they are critical tools.

Integrate your communications – voice, fax and e-mail – through a single modem; a separate fax number looks more impressive.

Arrange appropriate insurance and check that your household insurance will cover your business equipment.

Have on-site warranties for your equipment, with next-day repair.

Do not rely on the computer's hard disk alone. Make sure there's a backup.

Install a separate telephone line or convert your existing line to two lines to avoid family friction; make sure you have broadband internet.

As far as possible, gear your working time to accord with your prime time. Self-discipline is essential. Be assertive with private callers during the working day.

If working at home does not work for you, admit it and seek alternative employment.

11

Handling interruptions

It is hoped that, with all modern improvements, a way will be discovered of getting rid of bores, for it is too bad that... no punishment can be inflicted on those who steal your time and with it your temper and patience, as well as the bright thoughts that might have entered your mind if they had not been frightened away by the bore.

Lord Byron

Business people in most cases have highly fragmented working days. According to one study by Henry Mintzberg, Cleghorn Professor of Management Studies at McGill University in Montreal, senior managers spend half their time on activities to which they devote nine minutes or less – a far cry from the textbook model by which people plan and use their working day in blocks of coolly deliberate time. Mintzberg and others who have undertaken similar studies do not look upon these brief bouts of activity as time being frittered away. On the contrary, they conclude that results are achieved by talking with people: by listening, asking questions and possibly prodding for results.

But not all executives are proponents of what is termed 'management by walking around' (MBWA); even those who use this method require intervening periods of uninterrupted concentration. Hence strategies have to be devised to deal with the two prime causes of interruptions: drop-in visitors and the telephone (dealt with in its own right in Chapter 15).

Management by walking around

The advantages claimed for this style of management include:

- by keeping in touch with employees, the manager is kept informed about what is going on at the 'grass roots';

- employees feel cared for, which improves the work climate;
- conflict can be detected and defused before real problems arise.

Conversely, there can be some disadvantages, including:

- managers may spend too much time reacting to others and not enough time on planning;
- accessibility can create overload for the manager;
- employees can become unduly dependent upon their bosses to resolve their minor difficulties;
- employees may interpret it as micro-managing (or over-control).

The effect of the drop-in visitor

Most of the people who drop in to visit you at the office are likely to be colleagues, customers or suppliers, although with home-workers it may be their partner, children, a neighbour or a trades person.

Two factors that have contributed to the frequency of interruptions in conventional offices have been the growth in open-door managerial style, and open-plan office design. The latter has resulted from economic and environmental factors; space costs money and private offices are more expensive than open plan.

When interruptions become too numerous for effective working, it is useful to make a record of who interrupts, when and for what reason. This can be expanded, if necessary, to determine whether:

the visitors are wanted or unwanted;
they were invited or uninvited;
their interruption is regarded by you as a legitimate demand on your time, or a waste of it;
you feel you handled the interruption effectively.

As part of this analysis, it may be desirable to log the time spent with each drop-in visitor. Often you will find that the 80/20 rule (see Chapter 5) applies: ie 20 per cent of these visitors will take up 80 per cent of the total time taken up by all visitors. This may happen because these particular visitors have a tendency towards protracted socializing each time they visit you.

It may also be desirable to analyse what triggers the interruptions. The number of drop-in visitors may be high because of organizational faults due to confused responsibilities or misdirection of visitors; these may be described as accidental or easily explicable interruptions. On the other hand, a significant number of visitors may be self-generated and may necessitate a radical look at your own attitudes and behaviour. Such explanations could include:

- the lack of any plan for dealing with drop-ins;
- the feeling of importance they generate in you;
- your own enjoyment of socializing in office hours;
- a desire to be available: the 'ever-open door' syndrome;
- a fear of missing something on the information network;
- a lack of delegation;
- bad habits that have been allowed to develop uncorrected;
- inability to say no.

How to control interruptions

Where your analysis reveals that the number of drop-in visitors is a major problem for the organization generally, a top-level initiative may be required. One approach would be to establish a training programme to familiarize staff with the answers to constantly recurring questions. For example, it may be practical and cost-effective to train receptionists to answer customer enquiries. This would help to reduce the number of interruptions for the manager who previously had to handle these queries.

Another approach, and often the answer, is to plan your day to include a 'quiet hour' at certain specified times, during which interruptions are permitted only in very special circumstances. If, like many other people, you are at your most productive in the mornings, a suitable schedule might look like this:

08.00–08.30 contact with other staff;
08.30–09.30 quiet hour;
09.30–10.30 performance appraisal;
10.30–11.30 quiet hour;
11.30–12.30 meeting with client.

If this arrangement works for you, and is seen to be successful in coping with the problem, other managers may also decide to adopt it. Several organizations have even developed the idea to the point of making it part of company policy as regards internal telephone calls, as we will see in Chapter 15. Having a quiet-hour policy may not actually reduce the number of drop-in visitors, but it does enable people to have longer periods free from interruptions, and in which they can accomplish some constructive work.

There will be some situations where a quiet hour cannot be operated. Implementation may be more difficult when flexitime is worked, but variations may be possible even then.

For instance, in a team of four colleagues, one could handle all interruptions and safeguard the other three during the first hour, followed by the second person for the second hour, and so on.

The following is a list of other personal strategies that can help secure freedom from interruptions:

Close your door (if you have one). If you usually work with an open door, close it whenever you wish to be undisturbed. This will deter passers-by and corridor wanderers from dropping in. Alternatively, have a system of green and red lights to indicate your availability or non-availability.

Operate surgery hours. Even if a quiet hour cannot be operated throughout the organization, individuals can unilaterally (or preferably with the agreement and support of colleagues) arrange to see others only at certain predetermined times, similar to the way in which a doctor sees patients.

Make appointments with yourself. Direct reports may fill your diary with appointments to see other people, so why not make an appointment to be with yourself? This can effectively block out certain periods in which you can ensure that you are free from interruptions so that you can get on with work that requires periods of concentration.

Concentration

Concentration has two dimensions: depth and duration. Most of us take about ten minutes to get deeply focused and can then sustain concentration for about 20 minutes. After that we often need to take a break. In consequence we are really effective for only about half our time. Therefore, if deep concentration can be built up for 40 minutes at a stretch, prime productive time is increased and productivity improved.

With practice, it is possible to learn to concentrate faster by using the following methods:

Tackle only one thing at a time. When a thought intrudes into your concentration do not fight it, as this can create tension. Instead, acknowledge it is there, writing it down if necessary, then return to the task in hand.

Set a minimum time for staying on the task. Make an effort to complete it within that time. If you do not succeed, try to complete the particular stage you are engaged in before breaking off and switching to some other activity.

Reward yourself. Give yourself some tangible recognition, eg a walk around the block, to signify that you have increased your powers of concentration.

Have a hideaway. There are occasions when you may find it more convenient to do your important work away from your own office. The boardroom or the office of an absent colleague may be available, or you may decide to work at home. You could even sit in your car in the car park to get 15 minutes or so free from interruptions. In short, work in any place where you cannot be found, so that you cannot be interrupted.

Change your working hours. To obtain uninterrupted time, some people stay late at the office. Unfortunately, this is often unprofitable. There will always be someone who will drop in at the end of their day, often to kill time. A much more effective strategy is to arrive early; not only is it unlikely that others will be around, but you may find that travelling to the office is quicker than usual because of less traffic congestion – and the phone does not ring either!

Where interruptions to your concentration are unavoidable, prepare to pick up as soon as possible by taking ten seconds to jot down a brief reminder of where you have reached and by timing the interruption.

Whenever possible, it is better if others know in advance when you plan to make yourself unavailable – this can save their time as well as your own. There are almost certainly some parts of the day when interruptions are unavoidable; that is the time to programme shorter tasks that require only small blocks of time.

Other ways of reducing drop-in visits

Apart from the techniques to control time and place that we have already referred to, there are other tactics you can use to reduce the number of occasions when people make unscheduled visits to your office. One of these is to make a point of sharing your coffee break with those colleagues who may need to see you fairly frequently. Many points they may require to discuss with you can crop up during these so-called break periods, and time is thereby saved for all concerned. A variation is to schedule a meeting for 10.15 preceded by coffee at 10.00. Colleagues then have up to 15 minutes to socialize and discuss miscellaneous work issues before the meeting begins.

Effective screening is particularly important. Train your direct report so that when they are asked if you are busy, they can offer either to interrupt you or to request you to call the individual later. If the individual asks that you call them, the direct report should then follow up with, 'Can I do anything to assist?' Often the individual will respond by indicating the nature of their business, and the direct report may then be able to supply the information required or assemble the required papers for when you are free to call back and deal with the matter. Make sure your direct report asks when the caller will be available to receive your call.

The effect of office layout

With a little rearrangement, offices can be made inviting or uninviting to passers-by. Visitors are less likely to drop in if you position your desk so that you have your back to the entrance. Although some artefacts can be conducive to good staff management because they put people at ease and facilitate conversation, avoid making your office too comfortable or filling it with interesting gimmicks, otherwise your colleagues may see it as a social centre and drop in more frequently.

Another way of discouraging visiting time wasters is to hang up discouraging notices such as, 'If you have nothing to do, please don't do it here.' Make a point of visiting the other person's office when you have business to discuss with them. Apart from the benefits of the exercise in walking there and back, this leaves you in control of how long you stay there, which is much easier than trying to prise visitors out of your own office when they have overstayed their welcome. Alternatively, if your room happens to have an outer office or lobby, meet the visitors there. This makes it easier to withdraw into your inner sanctum to signify that the discussion is at an end.

Strategies for handling the unwanted visitor

When the unwanted visitor has finally reached your office despite all the above precautions, there are further strategies you can adopt to reduce the duration of the visit. Some of these are:

- Strategies related to seating. Have files and other paraphern-
alia on all the chairs. People are generally reluctant to remove
articles in order to sit down, and usually leave earlier if forced
to stand. Stand up yourself when you feel it is time for the
visitor to leave; this is an unmistakable signal. Or remain
standing yourself throughout the visit; people usually take
the hint and realize that you must be busy.
- Other non-verbal messages. Keep your pen poised throughout
the meeting as if you are in the middle of writing something.
Continue to look at the screen of your computer with your
fingers on the keyboard. Keep the phone in your hand as if
you were about to make a call.
- Avoid eye contact with unwelcome visitors. This makes them
feel uncomfortable and creates difficulty in maintaining the
conversation.
- Avoid socializing. Most interruptions have three distinct
parts: the introductory socializing, the reason for the interruption and the final socializing. The socializing is often more
time consuming than the reason for the visit. So cut down or
eliminate the introductory socializing and try to get straight to
the point.

Controlling the duration

Not all drop-in visitors are totally unwelcome, even though the
timing may be unfortunate and the intrusion into your planned
day a necessary nuisance. So indicate at the start of the meeting
how much time you can make available, by some phrase such as,
'Fred, I have 20 minutes, is that enough for your purpose?' If Fred
says yes, you have then established the boundary. Arrange for
your PA to phone you at the end of that time to indicate that your
next appointment, real or fictitious, is due.

If the conversation is slow in getting to the point, search for
a reason behind the visit. If this is not readily forthcoming try
saying, 'Fred, I sense that you're worried about something; would
you care to tell me what it is?' Be direct throughout the encounter

and stay in control. When the appointed time is nearly up, say, 'You'll have to excuse me in a minute or two, Fred, as there are other matters requiring my time.' Before Fred leaves it may be desirable to suggest that in future he should do one or more of the following:

- send an e-mail: this may remove the need for a meeting;
- give advance notice of the reason for his visit;
- sharpen up his own preparation;
- visit only during your 'surgery hours'.

However, such manipulation can sometimes be overdone. It must be remembered that a degree of ruthlessness with time is necessary but this should not be at the expense of offending people. Always mix your firmness with courtesy and don't forget the other side of the coin. There may be many occasions when it is important for you to interrupt others when they are very busy. Wouldn't it be dreadful if you were always made to feel unwelcome?

12

Managing information

After me, the deluge.

Attributed to Madame de Pompadour,
favourite of Louis XV of France

Many consultants have been called on to investigate the work of managers. Their conclusions show that a large number of executives do not work a productive 40-hour week. They work productively for 20 hours and spend the rest of their time in what can be much less productive activities unless effectively handled, namely handling information, increasingly in the form of e-mails or meetings.

Information comes from three sources:

oral;
written;
electronic.

Where information overload is a problem, this may arise from personal factors, organizational factors or how information is managed.

Personal factors

These can include inefficiency of the recipient, including procrastination and fear of making a decision, poor organization, such as not dealing with one task at a time and completing it, and lack of time.

To avoid information overload, learn to take control. Some ways to achieve this include:

- be selective in choosing to whom you give your contact details;
- learn to prioritize your messages and, if possible, have your PA do this for you;

- leave a message on your voicemail asking callers not to leave a message unless it must be dealt with today;
- ask them to ensure their messages are brief but detailed and indicate what action is required;
- ask your callers to speak slowly and distinctly;
- devise your own strategies to deal with the problem – it is in your best interests to do so;
- Learn also to respect other people's time and encourage them to reciprocate.

Organizational factors

These can include:

- **organizational culture:** where there is a blame culture, this can cause people to generate and distribute a lot of information to 'cover their backs';
- **excessive bureaucracy:** this may be internal and external;
- **multitasking:** where this is used, the volume of information to be handled is increased;
- **ineffective use of information technology:** over hundreds of years people have become wedded to paper. It offers flexibility, versatility, permanence and disposability. It is also cheap and everyone can use it. But for archiving, searching and the transmission of data, technology should be used.

There will always be some people who will oppose reduction in paperwork. Having a steady flow of paper crossing their desk gives them a sense of accomplishment. It can also be used for self-protection and giving a sense of security by preserving the appearance of high activity. Additionally, paper is easier to manage than people; so they can use sorting paper as an excuse for not doing their real job.

Other people tackle the problem more effectively. Witness how Bill Gates works. He uses three linked 21-inch monitors. Similarly, more organizations are tackling the problem. Airlines are a good example: passengers can book online and download their own boarding passes.

At the same time, many governments appear oblivious to the costly bureaucratic burdens they impose on organizations by excessive legislation. Few organizations seek to quantify such costs but those that do so are appalled by the figure.

Managing information on paper

Organizations individually may be able to do little to combat the deluge of government-generated paperwork. However, it is possible to reduce the flow of information generated within the organization. When this is undertaken it usually reveals evidence of uneconomic duplication of work.

Dealing with paper requires an effective system that:

- eliminates unnecessary paper;
- avoids generating unnecessary paper;
- establishes a location for essential paper;
- creates a method for easy paper retrieval.

Among the ways to achieve this are:

- control the photocopier;
- give people an incentive to control paper, particularly e-mails (no hard copies unless essential);
- seek to avoid the use of paper in discussions.

As a first step in reducing paperwork, the flow of paper should be tracked. Find out where each piece originates, the offices through which it passes and how it is finally completed. When you have a clear picture of how each piece of paper flows, you will find it possible to plan more effective control in the future. Begin by asking some fundamental questions, such as how much it costs to produce the information generated. Once the high cost is known, this could encourage the organization to reduce its volume.

> ## Don't move the safe
>
> Within a year, Marks & Spencer was able to eliminate 26 million cards and sheets of paper weighing 120 tons. This achievement resulted partly from trusting people more and partly from 'sensible approximation': getting figures close enough for all practical purposes is more efficient than striving for exactitude. There is no point in spending ten pence to move the safe in order to recover the five-pence coin that has rolled under it.

As a recipient you can ensure more effective reports by asking yourself:

Do I need this report? If not, ask the sender to remove your name from the distribution list.

Does the report arrive on time? If it is consistently late, take steps to ensure that the sender rectifies the situation or eliminates the report. Also check if the deadline for the report is arbitrary.

Is the report too detailed? Do you need figures to the third decimal point or would rounded-up estimates be good enough?

Is there too much information? Ensure that only pertinent data are included.

Is the format action-oriented? Problems, opportunities and actions should be clearly set out.

Is there an executive summary at its beginning?

For your own reports, first find out:

- who reads them;
- who really uses them;
- whether similar information is available elsewhere or being compiled by someone else.

Using the same approach, critically examine the journals and periodicals circulating in your department. Can the information be collected and disseminated more effectively by some other method? For example:

- Would it be more efficient to telephone or meet someone in person, in preference to getting written information?
- Rather than sending out masses of emails, would a monthly or quarterly newsletter be preferable, to keep employees abreast of changes, progress towards goals and so on; further, would it be acceptable to have this newsletter available in electronic format only?
- Should you send out just one copy and have it routed to a number of recipients or pin it on a notice board?
- Can the information be collated and disseminated more effectively by some other method?

Another technique is to try suspending simultaneously all reports for a month, allowing only those to return which managers demand after living without them for that length of time.

Beyond a certain point, however, reducing paperwork can be counterproductive. For example, the colleague who previously refined their ideas on paper before circulating the document may be tempted to drop in and think the ideas through in your office. In that case, though there may be a saving in paperwork, you may lose even more time.

When designing or introducing any new hard-copy form, make a careful examination of the need for it by asking:

- Is it really necessary; is there an existing form that can be modified?
- What other forms can be eliminated as a result of its introduction?
- How much training time will be required to bring it into use?
- What will it cost to use the form, and will its benefits exceed its cost?
- Could this form be completed online? If so, design an electronic form.

Send fewer and better letters

To seek to reduce the number of letters you write, ask yourself:

Need I write at all?
Can I put a note on my business card instead of sending a covering letter?
Can I telephone instead of writing?
Would a routing slip suffice?
Could I write a reply on the original letter, indicating that I have kept a copy where appropriate?
Could I send an e-mail?

Also ask whether you can make use of any of the following form of letters:

- speed-letter forms, ie three-part notes combining message, response and copy;
- pre-printed standard letters, which require only the addition of date, name, address, salutation and signature, with a few blank spaces;
- guide letters, which are complete letters that are not pre-printed but which supply specimen phrases that can be changed to fit any occasion.

In addition to saving time, the form letters have the advantage of facilitating prompter replies, correct statements of policy, etc. They are usually better written, require fewer copies and cost less than ordinary letters.

When it is necessary for policy or courtesy reasons to write an ordinary letter, you can save time by:

- trying to keep it down to one or two sentences or a single paragraph;
- avoiding quoting points back which the originator has already made at length; refer to them by number instead;
- checking that all the points have been answered in your reply.

A high proportion of people read all their outgoing letters before signing them; with a direct report this should not be needed. Keep at hand for reference a list of words that are commonly misspelt. Those who prepare letters for you should have and use spellcheck software (while being aware of its limitations!).

The one-word letter

A consultant sought to illustrate to a group of business people effective letters containing one sentence each. Shortly afterwards he received a letter reading:

> Dear X
> Thanks.
> Yours sincerely
> J Smith

For several years the consultant displayed the letter at his talks to show that one word could be a complete communication, also stating that one word had to be an absolute minimum. Then he received another letter:

> Dear X
> Appreciatively yours
> R Evans

Similarly, when a landlord gave a tenant notice to leave, the tenant replied:

> Dear X
> I remain
> Yours sincerely
> A Robens

Every piece of paper or the information on it can be managed effectively when put to use in one of the following places:

- wastepaper basket;
- calendar;
- reference file;
- miscellaneous file;
- action file.

If you have an assistant, train them to:

- discard papers of no interest before they reach you;
- ask for your name to be deleted from the circulation lists of reports that are no longer relevant to you;
- route appropriate mail directly to your support staff;
- answer routine mail enquiries on your behalf, using form letters wherever possible;
- file any information that needs to be retained and requires no action now;
- underline or highlight the main points of letters and periodicals that require your attention;
- assemble relevant information to assist your replies.

You can make things a lot easier for yourself by insisting that any written problem sent for your attention is always accompanied by a suggested answer. You can also make marginal notes as you read an incoming letter or memo and leave it to your assistant to frame the reply. Where appropriate, you can even write your reply in legible longhand on the incoming letter, mailing it back to the sender with a label attached saying:

> Speed reply. In this instance we believe you will prefer speed to formality. In order to give you the fastest possible response, we have written these marginal notes as our reply. A copy has been kept.

Speeding the action

Where your personal attention is required, your paperwork should be sorted into two categories:

Information only, eg inter-office memos that can be read when you have five minutes between appointments;
unimportant: if you ignore it or put it on one side you may find that the need to handle it disappears.

Make it a rule to try to handle each piece of paper only once and to determine its destiny immediately. Failure to act will double the time spent on it when you handle it again.

As we suggested in Chapter 10, one way of checking how well you do this is by putting a pencilled dot in the top corner of every piece of paper as you pick it up. An apparent dose of smallpox (a multiplicity of dots) is then a measure of your paper-shuffling tendencies.

If you have to retain a letter for further information, before replying put it in a pending file; don't leave it cluttering your desk. In many cases paper is postponed decisions.

Whenever paperwork begins to pile up, try to schedule a half day free from interruption to enable you to clear the backlog. Far more can be accomplished at one sitting than by handling it piecemeal.

If additional work is created for you because others delay in replying, you can follow up by:

- sending them a brief handwritten note asking if you have missed their reply;
- enclosing a stamped addressed envelope;
- using a speed-letter form as a reminder with built-in alternative replies prepared;
- writing on stationery with a few blank lines at the bottom, inviting your correspondent to write a reply in the space provided;
- sending a photocopy of your original letter with a reminder slip attached:

> Reminder. Your reply to the original of the attached copy hasn't reached me yet. Please re-read this copy and give me your urgent response.

■ getting your assistant to telephone the addressee's direct report to check progress; the letter may have gone astray in the post.

Filing and finding papers

A poor filing system can be a monumental time waster, yet filing frequently suffers from a lack of planning. Witness the manner in which filing procedures are still often left to the whim of the raw recruit rather than to well-trained personnel.

The volume of paper will be reduced by some of the letter-writing methods already mentioned, but as a final check before filing, ask yourself, 'If I wanted this again and did not have it, what would I do?' Depending on the answer, filing may not be necessary after all.

The retention of filed material is best determined by use and importance rather than by arbitrary rules. Some papers, in particular legal documents, must be retained for the life of the organization, whereas others should never be kept at all. Managers should always be concerned with the future; they are not employed as archivists delving into history.

To misquote Longfellow:

> Lives of great men all remind us,
> As we their pages turn,
> That we too may leave behind us
> Letters that we ought to burn.

When paper must be filed, it may be desirable to put a destruction date on it. No medals are handed out for the development of a filing system for obsolete memos. Items that will be of value for a short period only should be placed in a temporary store.

Filing systems should be capable of being easily understood and readily accessible. The cost of filing equipment is often low when compared with the cost of time taken to find missing documents; hence it is desirable to have enough separate files so that each item has only one logical destination. It is better to start a new file than to stick an item in with a distant relative. However, avoid the other extreme of having hundreds of subdivisions with only one or two items in each file. Files should be numbered and a separate index kept with file titles and reference numbers. Scanning such a list to ascertain a file number is less cumbersome than searching through the filing cabinets.

There are many simple devices that can be used for temporary filing, eg spikes, clips and divider cards in a box. They may not look elegant but can be cheap and efficient.

A set of temporary working files may also be useful. These can be labelled:

urgent and important;
for review: important but not urgent;
to do: routine.

Hyperactive files should be retained near at hand. They may be kept in a drawer of your desk and should be clearly labelled and organized for quick and easy access.

Nowadays most items should not be stored in paper form. Electronic storing is much superior in terms of cost and efficiency. Bear in mind that 17 trees must be felled to produce one ton of the lowest grade of newsprint; an acre of trees is needed for just one day's issue of a newspaper. So electronic storing produces an enormous ecological saving as well as reducing the colossal amount of time we all spend on reading and shuffling documents.

In short, an effective information-management system:

eliminates unnecessary information;
avoids generating unnecessary further information;
establishes a system for storing essential information;
creates a method for easy retrieval of information.

13

Making your reading and writing more effective

Some books are to be tasted, others swallowed, and some few to be chewed and digested.

Francis Bacon

Much time is wasted at work because two of the 'three Rs' we learnt at school are sadly neglected: the skills of reading and writing. We tend to take them for granted in later life but fail to update them to suit the changed context in which we work. As we saw in Chapter 12, paper pollutes our lives. We live in an age of information overload but with a shortage of real communication. Before reading or writing anything we need to ask ourselves, 'Will this help me to achieve my goals?' If the answer is 'No,' do not deal with it.

Managing your reading load

For many of us the first step towards a reading-time improvement plan is to dump. It may also be possible to get your name off some mailing lists. If so, do it. If not, dump junk mail.

Wherever possible, a busy person should delegate reading to others. There are always some people who revel in reading and are prepared to dig around to find those items that are likely to be of interest and relevance to you. If you cannot find a 'natural' to do this for you, perhaps you can instruct and train your direct report to do so as a routine part of their job. Spouses and partners can sometimes be useful in this respect also, or even children with a thirst for new knowledge.

Professional journals and learned papers can be routed directly to one of your staff, who can highlight items that they think you should see.

Alternatively, you and your colleagues may agree to share the monitoring of specific publications so that everybody does not have to read everything. The benefits of such an arrangement are that the people most likely to be interested get first look at any information crucial to their work and can then quickly circulate relevant items to others concerned, thereby keeping the whole team informed.

Prioritizing and streamlining your professional reading

Professional or 'active' reading – seeking out key publications and sources of information – is far more fruitful than merely reading passively by relying on general-interest publications and publicity materials that just happen to land on your desk.

It can be salutary to ask yourself, 'Would I subscribe to this journal if I had to pay for it?' If the answer is 'No,' remove your name from the mailing list.

When professional reading is necessary, it should be given an order of priority. Ask yourself:

Which are the best papers, periodicals, professional journals and books for me to read?
Who looks at the subject from a different standpoint?
What are my competent colleagues currently reading?
What information is available on the internet?

If you can neither delegate nor share the reading load, it may be worthwhile to subscribe to a good abstracting service, a good newsletter service in your particular field or an internet site. Such services are usually concise, readable and rich in information.

Another way of reducing your reading load is by using your ears to assimilate information. For example, you can always listen to a CD or MP3 when travelling to and from work.

Adjusting your reading style and speed

It is important to treat reading as a skill in its own right that needs to be learnt and practised. To take new material on board more efficiently, you should first glance through it fairly quickly, concentrating on the summary and/or contents list to get a general grasp. On the basis of this you can then decide which method of reading to use:

Skimming: skipping through each section to spot the main ideas and obtain a general picture of the contents to determine which parts, if any, you should read more carefully. This can be supplemented by reading the preface or introduction, and then the first and last sentences of each paragraph.

Scanning: searching to find answers to particular questions that interest you. Let your eyes take in several lines at a time until key words or phrases begin to jump out at you. A rapid diagonal search of each page in the form of a large letter Z is an efficient method for rapidly scanning a large book.

Intensive reading: careful word-by-word reading when you want to understand arguments fully, memorize facts, prepare for a detailed discussion or master a new subject. It is important to avoid the bad habit of mentally sounding each word as you read it; this adds nothing to comprehension and merely slows down your visual intake.

Critical reading: searching for inconsistencies and looking for inaccuracies, such as when checking a draft text or preparing to write a review.

Other practical hints to enable you to improve your reading efficiency and retention include:

- Adjust your reading speed according to the fog index (see later in this chapter) or difficulty level of the material you are trying to assimilate.
- Do not attempt to read technical material for more than an hour at a time.

- At intervals review in your mind what you have just read, then read on and again review all that you have read since you started the session. These progressive reviews will help to retain the material in your mind.
- Put what you have just read to practical use at the earliest possible opportunity. If you are reading something that you may have to refer back to later, make it easier for yourself by highlighting or underlining the most relevant portions; otherwise make brief notes of those items that are of most significance to you.
- You may consider it worthwhile to take a speed-reading course. Some people obtain great benefit from such courses, which often claim to double your reading speed and enable improved comprehension. Their essential advice includes:
  - Do not move your eyes from side to side as you read each line; this will help develop your peripheral vision and saves energy.
  - Avoid vocalizing, ie mouthing or mentally speaking the words as you read them with your eyes.
  - Do not re-read or backtrack.
  - Increase your reading span; try to take in groups of words rather than single words each time you shift your focus.
  - Use a pencil or finger to draw your eyes down the page slightly faster than they would move naturally. They will soon adjust to this and you can progressively increase your speed.
  - Start with the second or third word of each line, thereby avoiding wasting your peripheral vision on the margin.

Many people find it difficult to use speed reading when dealing with a schedule of figures. With figures:

- read the heading across the top;
- read the lines down the side;
- check any notes at the bottom of the page;
- decide the key figures you need and look at them; if they are not contentious, ignore the rest.

Remember, however, that your primary objective is to be not just a speed reader but a speed understander.

Additionally, do not overlook the alternative to a speed-reading course, which is to persuade some of your colleagues to attend a course in effective writing to encourage brevity in the reports they submit for your attention.

A reading-time improvement plan

To keep track of your progress as a more time-effective reader, make an analysis from time to time of the savings you are making on the various types of reading material that need your attention. A suggested form for this is given in Table 13.1.

Table 13.1 Reading-time improvement plan: analysis form

Material	Time taken per week	Time saved by:			Total
		eliminating	delegating	better method	
letters					
memos					
newspapers					
periodicals					
journals					
books					
e-mails					
internet					
other					
Total					

Keeping reading under control

Never allow your reading tasks to build up to an unreasonable level. If necessary, earmark a specified period daily for reading. If you have not managed to read a particular item by a specific target date, discard it. Keeping yourself informed does not mean reading last year's or even last month's ideas today. But do keep a special file for retaining items of particular interest, and at an appropriate time read all those accumulated on a particular topic. You are more likely to retain information by reading widely on one subject at a single sitting than by gathering snatches of information piecemeal on the same subject at irregular intervals.

Where, when and how to do your reading may also require thought:

Where. Many managers feel guilty about reading at their office desk; they see it as unproductive or even as not working at all. Yet there are specific advantages to reading at your desk rather than in an armchair or on a couch: you will have at hand the necessary materials – paper, pens, highlighters, clips – for dealing actively with the subject matter.

When. Reading during normal office hours may not be the best answer because of distractions. If this is so, consider going in early or staying late in order to increase the chances of ensuring uninterrupted attention to this important aspect of your managerial duties; or arrange to take the reading matter with you on a long train or air journey.

How. This may be a matter of personal choice or habit, but do not get too comfortable and have the reading material at an angle of 45 degrees. The more comfortable you are, the less your concentration and capacity for retention.

More effective writing

Writing in longhand as opposed to using your computer is in itself a great time waster; yet some managers are still reluctant to master the skill of typing, preferring to stick to the time-consuming established methods of written drafts.

The more you depend on written communication, the greater the demands you make on the time of others who will have to process it, read it and then possibly spend further time querying its meaning or intention. This may well rebound on you, the originator, leading to further consumption of your precious time. For this reason it is important that your written communications should be simple, understandable and to the point. The suggestions that follow provide some illustrations of the value of brevity in communication if the result is to be worth remembering.

Words should be used to communicate and clarify. Think how ridiculous it would be if the following well-known sayings were expressed in the kind of pompous officialese so widespread in business and government:

> Collated behavioural tendencies of homo sapiens reveal that defunct members of the masculine gender characteristically abstain from communicative transferral of anecdotal disclosures. (Dead men tell no tales.)
>
> The degree of force exerted that will impact on bodies which have descended suddenly from above is directly proportional to the size in volume terms of these same bodies. (The bigger they are, the harder they fall.)
>
> The diurnal intake of fruit in the form of the species *pomum vulgaris* has a pronounced repulsive effect on the attendance of registered medical practitioners. (An apple a day keeps the doctor away.)

Civil servants and lawyers in particular are often reluctant to use less than 25 words when one would do; this has been amusingly parodied in the TV series *Yes, Minister*, and has been accepted as being very near the truth. Here is a real-life example from the Education (School of Governing Bodies) Regulations 1981 Number 2 (3), which states:

> In these regulations any reference to a Regulation is a reference to a Regulation of these Regulations, any reference in a Regulation to a paragraph is a reference to a paragraph of that Regulation, and any reference in a paragraph to a sub-paragraph is a reference to a sub-paragraph of that paragraph.

Presumably this was originally written in a well-intentioned attempt to clarify, but it seems to have had the opposite effect, further muddying some already murky waters.

Much of this type of archaic language has been inherited from our 19th-century ancestors. Flowery verbose language was then a symbol of literacy and there is still a lot of this unnecessary verbiage around. This should not, however, be used as an excuse for indulging in it ourselves.

We are all tempted from time to time to strive for verbal elegance rather than simple words and ease of communication, so perhaps we should call to mind that the Lord's Prayer has only 57 words, the Ten Commandments 297, and the American Declaration of Independence 300.

Expressiveness versus pomposity

It can be a salutary experience to ask your colleagues, 'What do I do that wastes your time?' Often the answer will relate to written work: you can save the time of others by writing less and communicating more. Your aim should be to *express*, not to *impress*.

Check your e-mails and correspondence: are they as clear and concise as they should be? If you write to your loved one to say, 'I enjoyed kissing you,' you would never express the sentiment as: 'I found our osculatory connection to be a most pleasant sensation.' So why write in similar pompous language to your business colleagues? Maybe this particular example will help you to remember to apply the KISS principle in your business correspondence: Keep It Short and Simple.

Particularly avoid creating status-enhancing memos with printed headings such as 'From the desk of...'. Such self-glorification does not impress others and merely raises the risk of ridicule or parody with a reply beginning, 'Dear Desk' or 'I do not correspond with items of office furniture.' The ultimate idiocy is when you have two 'desks' corresponding with each other.

When to use a long word and when not

When the correct word to express a particular idea is a long one, by all means use it; but if you can find a shorter one that does the same job, use it in preference. Whole forests go under the chainsaw annually so that self-important managers can 'finalize the termination' of something, rather than just ending it.

Table 13.2 lists some common expressions to avoid, with suitable substitutes.

Table 13.2 Simple expressions are best

Avoid these expressions	Use these instead
ascertain	find out
acquire	get
acquaint with	tell
at this point in time	now
fully cognizant of	know
hold in abeyance	wait
commence	start, begin
despatch	send

Mark Twain had the right idea when he said, 'I never write metropolis for seven cents when I can get the same price for city.'

Your typing can also be done a lot more quickly if you use simple words; there are 18 character strokes in 'fully cognizant of' compared with only four in 'know'.

(The authors accept that the reader may now search this book for examples of our failure to keep to the required standard!)

Some tips for polishing your writing

Think through what you want to say and to whom. If necessary, jot down an outline. Ask yourself, 'Why do I want someone to read this?' Omit preliminaries and try to make the first sentence the most interesting and compelling, as newspaper columnists do.

Paragraphs are a form of punctuation, so separate your thoughts by packaging them in paragraphs. The paragraph is the basic building block of a letter or report, and the toughest part for many writers is to prevent each paragraph running on and on.

A sentence should express a single idea clearly. Keep your sentences short. However, some long sentences are easy to read if they are built around one idea.

Exercise care with punctuation. Understand how to use commas. They can change the meaning of a sentence completely. Note the effect of the commas in: 'Managers, whose minds are dull, do not get promotion.' What was meant was: 'Managers whose minds are dull do not get promotion'.

Careless punctuation once caused an expensive embarrassment for a supervisor at an American government nuclear installation. He ordered rods of radioactive material to be cut into 'ten foot long lengths' and got ten pieces each a foot long instead of the ten-foot lengths required.

Use the active voice. You are ducking responsibility if you begin your sentences with such passive circumlocutions as 'It is considered that...' or 'It is recommended that...'. This is vulgarly known as 'cover your anatomy' writing, which relies on irresolute language: little people using big words to leave room for ambiguity and possible escape if they should be proved wrong or are challenged.

Use active verbs. The verb 'to be' in all its forms (am, are, were, been) reinforces the status quo and creates only passive responses. In particular, beginning a sentence with 'There are...' often indicates the beginning of bad writing habits. Don't write 'There are carpets covering all the floors' when you can use the more active form, 'Carpets cover all the floors'.

Similarly, avoid constructions such as 'Reports will be submitted in writing and will be mailed to reach Head Office by the first of each month,' when you can give stronger direction by saying, 'Mail your reports to reach Head Office by the first of each month'.

Write positive statements whenever possible. Negative statements take longer to write, are harder to understand and generate inactive responses. Double negatives are just ungrammatical: 'I didn't do nothing.'

Don't nominalize, ie avoid adding '...tion' or '...ment' to a verb to turn it into a static noun. At all costs avoid such expressions as 'utilization' when you simply mean 'use'.

Weed out dangling present participles: words ending in '…ing'. These verbal adjectives can puzzle your readers when you place them wrongly or leave them suspended in mid-sentence, such as in 'Walking through one district of Paris, the Eiffel Tower dominates the whole area.' This sentence implies that the Eiffel Tower was doing the walking – a highly unlikely event. The golden rule for avoiding this type of ambiguity is that a participle at the beginning of a sentence must always have a noun or pronoun on which to lean.

Avoid splitting the subject from its object or verb. For example, 'The document was filed by the employee who was working on it in the wrong drawer' should have been written as 'The document was filed in the wrong drawer by the employee who was working on it.'

Take care with pronouns and remove all doubt about the nouns for which they stand, otherwise you could have a sentence such as 'If the baby does not thrive on cold milk, boil it.'

Avoid organizational 'gobbledygook'. This term was invented in the 1940s by US congressman Maury Maverick to describe the language of bureaucrats. Some bureaucrats or public relations executives frequently manage to put themselves on record without really saying anything meaningful. They use circumlocution and euphemisms to turn 'explosion' into 'energetic disassembly', 'fire' into 'rapid oxidation' and 'plutonium contamination' into 'plutonium taking up residence'. This is really an indirect form of lying but it is more than likely that such people would call a lie a 'terminological inexactitude' and see no harm in it.

Finally, remember the alleged motto of the Royal College of Surgeons: 'If in doubt, cut it out.' Why not do the same with your words?

Readability tests and the fog index

Various tests have been devised to determine the readability of printed or written material. Among these are the Cloze Procedure, the Dale-Chall Formula, the Flesch Formula and the Gunning Fog Index. The last-named is the most widely used. Its objective is to encourage writing that has a fog index of no more than six.

To determine the fog index of your writing:

1   Choose at random a paragraph of your writing that is about 120 words long. Count the number of words in each sentence and calculate the average. Treat any clearly independent clauses as separate sentences, eg 'In school we read, we learn, we improve' counts as three sentences, not one.

2   Count the number of words with three or more syllables, excluding:
     – capitalized words;
     – combinations of shorter words, eg chainsaw;
     – verbs in the present or past tense that reach a third syllable because of the addition of -ed or -es;
     – the first word of each sentence.

3   Add the average sentence length to the polysyllable word count, and multiply the total by 0.4. The resulting number is reckoned to be the years of schooling needed to understand what you have written. A score of 17 or more means that the prose is so densely wrapped in fog that only graduates could grope their way through it.

Written material can be categorized into:

light: this includes modern fiction, popular magazines and the tabloid daily and Sunday papers;
average: trade journals and hobby publications;
heavy: any technical material with which you are not familiar, or literature written in previous centuries.

Good advice when reading is to vary your reading speed according to the fog index level and to take the heavier material at a slower pace.

How interesting

In addition to producing a table for computing 'reading ease', Rudolf Flesch devised a 'human-interest score' which operates as follows:

1   Use samples of 100 words.
2   In each sample, count the personal words, defined as all proper nouns denoting persons and all pronouns where antecedents are pronouns (you, we, they, he, them), but not 'it' or a plural pronoun referring to a thing. Count all words with gender, such as father or daughter, businessman, actress, and proper names, but not vocational nouns with common gender (doctor, teacher, barrister) and collective nouns such as people and team.
3   Count up your sample's personal sentences – any sentence containing speech set off by quotation marks or by references such as 'he said', sentences addressed directly to the reader as a question, command or suggestion, a sentence cast as an exclamation, or any incomplete sentence of a conversational nature.
4   Multiply the number of personal words in each 100-word sample by 3.635. Multiply the number of personal sentences by 0.314. Add the two products. The total is your human-interest score, which runs from a dull 5 through to interesting at 30 and dramatic at 80.

Remember: a readability formula is not a writing rule, but simply a tool to help you write the way you talk.

14

Active listening

Our maker gave us two ears and one tongue.

Anonymous

Many courses are available on effective reading, effective report writing and effective speaking. Comparatively few, however, are available on effective listening. This is surprising in view of the amount of time most people spend listening. Further, as most people are only about 25 per cent efficient as listeners, sizeable sums are paid to people to listen ineffectively and waste time.

Often a poor listener will:

- call a subject uninteresting;
- criticize the speaker's delivery;
- get over-stimulated by certain points;
- fake attention;
- tolerate distractions.

As a rule, poor listening is not the result of any one cause. Poor listening habits develop just as does poor posture in walking. In turn, poor listening leads to inefficiency, misunderstanding and conflict. It may also result in more things being put in writing. In turn this requires more staff, equipment and space; and information overload may result.

Progressive deafness

One measure used to test listening skill is the chain loss in oral communication experiment. This research tool is a variation of the old parlour game. Six participants are selected and five leave the room. The remaining person is shown a slide. It shows two people: a well-dressed black man and a white man wearing working clothes. They are involved in some sort of altercation. Also on the slide are a clock, some passive characters, some advertising display cards and a few other insignificant details. After studying the slide for two minutes, the first participant reports the scene to one of the other participants on their return to the room.

The process is repeated by that participant to the next person returning to the room, and so on until the chain is completed.

Distinct problems emerge. The first participant, fresh from their visual study of the slide's contents, gives the next person a fairly accurate report about the two central figures having some kind of altercation. That next person also relays much detail. However, as the story is repeated, the quantity of information is sharply reduced and the central theme is lost. The final participant gets a report with no mention of the altercation by the two central figures. 'Listening loss' obliterates the significant item. And even if the central theme does surface, it is usually distorted in the direction of previously held stereotypes. Using experiments of this kind, the immediate recall is usually of the order of 50 per cent. After 48 hours most listeners remember only about 25 per cent of what they heard.

Research among management personnel of General Electric in the United States revealed that:

- listening skills differ substantially between individuals;
- people can be trained to improve their listening skills;
- certain common pitfalls to good listening are identifiable.

Why listening skills differ

There are a number of reasons why listening skills can differ. For example, listening ability may be associated with problems of vocabulary. It would be difficult for a non-economist to follow a lecturer who uses the following terminology:

> My lecture this morning is devoted to the examination of an economy in which the second derivatives of the utility function

possess a finite number of discontinuities. To keep the problem manageable, I assume that each individual consumes only two goods and dies after one Robertsonian week. Only elementary mathematical tools such as topology will be employed.

Local dialects can also present managers with difficulties. Witness London-based companies that have built plants in the north west of England. Initially a dialect expert is required to translate such everyday expressions as 'Intitut?' ('Isn't it hot?') and 'Eez gooinooam' ('He's going home').

Problems often arise if the views of the listener are rigid – one cause of ineffective listening among older persons especially. When a person's mind is made up, it will filter out the facts that go against cherished beliefs. Implications not intended by the speaker may also be invented. As evidence of this, listen to a discussion between a capitalist and a socialist or between a manager and a shop-floor representative.

It should also be recognized that there are different types of listening. Listening to a Beethoven symphony requires a specific skill: an ability to appreciate music. Listening effectively to a lecture on the process of photosynthesis requires understanding of information, ideas and relationships. Then again, different sets of listening skills are required when we listen with discrimination and critical judgement to a salesperson's pitch or the speech of a political candidate.

In Germany and Japan, because the verb is at the end of the sentence, people need to listen to the whole sentence and not try to finish it for the speaker.

The three processes

Effective listening involves three processes:

Hearing. This is the physical and neurological process that enables a person to hear sounds above a threshold intensity level within a certain frequency range.

Listening. This is being aware of auditory impact but without evaluation; the mind may be likened to a sponge that just absorbs sensory impressions.

Understanding. The message takes on meaning within the listener's frame of reference; understanding may come through empathy or by relating it to something of which the listener has knowledge.

Listening with understanding may be undermined by a number of factors, including:

Distractions from the environment. In view of the built-in psychological barriers to effective listening, the problems should not be compounded with easily avoidable environmental pitfalls. Accordingly:

- Shut out unnecessary noise.
- Ensure that there are no phone calls or other distractions such as drop-in visitors.
- Avoid doodling, tapping or shuffling papers around.
- Check that room temperature and humidity are right.
- Ensure that the communicating parties are in a condition to be attentive, eg they are not suffering from fatigue or headaches.

Distractions within the listener. People have built-in emotional filters that distort their listening process in a variety of ways including:

- **Defensiveness.** If what is heard appears threatening to the listener, attention may become focused on feelings rather than on what is being said.
- **Resentment.** When views are expressed that conflict with the listener's ideas, understanding and retention may be blocked because the listener is planning what to say in response. Or they may be classifying things as right or wrong, good or bad, instead of listening to all the evidence.
- **Reactions to the speaker.** If the listener does not like the speaker, their manner or appearance, or feels threatened by them, this can distort the listening process.

- **Priority focus.** When someone has an important meeting scheduled in 15 minutes or there is a pressing matter on their mind because of a priority, they may tune out the speaker and perhaps not hear them at all. This is particularly likely to be the case when the subject is not one that is of special interest.
- **Reactions to the subject.** If the subject is one with which the manager is not familiar or if it is not appealing, it is harder to concentrate than when the subject is interesting.
- **Halo effect.** The listener may so admire someone as to accept without question what they say.

Distractions arising from the speaker. These may be caused by such factors as:

- mannerisms;
- dress and/or grooming;
- use of language;
- style;
- accent.

Towards effective listening

Oral communication has two distinct parts: transmitting and receiving; or, more specifically, a speaker and a listener. The latter is the more important. This can be demonstrated by having an excellent speaker and a poor speaker present the same lecture to two groups of students, using the same material. If the students' motivation is comparable, they get almost as much from the poor lecturer as from the excellent one. In other words, listeners who are really willing to do their share can make up for poor delivery. Hence Emerson's statement, 'Tis the good reader that makes the good book' can be reworded, 'Tis the good listener that makes the good speech.'

To sharpen and upgrade our listening skills we should:

Listen to how things are said. The delivery of speech can be broken down into four components:

- **Emphasis.** This may be placed on different words in a sentence and add meaning. For example, place the emphasis on the italicized word in each of the following sentences:

  Bob, what was that?
  Bob, *what* was that?
  Bob, what *was* that?
  Bob, what was *that*?

- **Speed of delivery.** Variations from the individual's normal rate of speaking can give significant clues to the speaker's feelings. People tend to talk faster when angry, excited or frustrated, and more slowly when thinking or reluctant to discuss a topic.
- **Tone.** When there is stress or anxiety, often the throat muscles tighten and the voice moves to a higher pitch.
- **Volume.** An increase in speech volume usually indicates an increase in emotional intensity.

Observe non-verbal behaviour. A speaker does not communicate by words only. People are constantly moving, and their movements can reveal feelings, emotions and reactions. Indeed, appreciation of non-verbal behaviour is fundamental to intelligent listening. In particular, pay attention to:

- Eye contact. How one person looks at another is a major part of non-verbal communication.
- Use of hands. Next to movement of the eyes, movement of the hands present the most expressive non-verbal communication.
- Posture. How a person sits or stands can be a key indicator of factors such as their stress level and the degree of cooperation they are offering.

Use spare time effectively. A major cause of ineffective listening is the fact that a person can listen at a much faster rate that the speed at which thoughts can be converted to speech.

According to laboratory tests, people talk at rates of 100 to 200 words a minute and think at somewhere between 600 and 800 words a minute. How this spare capacity is used is a big factor in determining the degree of listening effectiveness. The effective listener uses the extra thinking time to review what the speaker has said, structuring the message and watching for meaningful non-verbal communications such as facial expressions and gestures. In the average untrained listener the reverse occurs. The brain engages in activities that impede comprehension; for example, it may be planning the afternoon work schedule. If this happens in, say, a meeting, the remarks of the last speaker are missed.

We should also be aware that we have a built-in emotional filter that distorts our listening process. If the topic in question is one that arouses deep-seated emotional reactions on the part of the listener, the poor listener does not concentrate on what is being said. Similarly, if the listener does not like the appearance or manner of the speaker, this too can distort the listening process. Linked with this is the use of emotionally charged words or words of a derogatory, racist, sexist or sectarian nature, such as those a racist or sexist might use. Our emotional filters may block such words or phrases when they enter the ear, or they may allow them to rush in with such force so that they are deeply impressed on our memory.

Listen with your eyes

As well as listening with your ears, listen with your eyes. Body language can reveal a great deal about what a person is saying. Catalogues of body language signals have been developed that describe the 'meaning' of different postures and gestures. For example:

Eye contact. People normally look at each other for 40–60 per cent of the time. More eye contact can reveal interest, while avoiding it may indicate disinterest or dislike.
Facial expressions. A smile, frown, puzzled look and nod are some of the expressions that communicate feelings of fear, anger, surprise, approval and boredom.

Position. Leaning towards or away from the speaker may indicate interest or lack of it by the listener.

Arms and legs. When crossed, they may indicate defensiveness or an unwillingness to change.

Hands. When open, and particularly when the person's coat is also open, these indicate openness.

Because body language is largely an unconscious form of communication, it is less likely to be manipulated or disguised. However, bear in mind that body language is culturally based.

Training to listen

A number of approaches have been tried to help people develop more effective listening habits. At the most basic level, we can offer a list of ten guidelines for good listening:

1   Stop talking! Nature gave you two ears and one tongue; take the hint.
2   Prepare yourself to listen. Listening is an active, not a passive, process.
3   Put the talker at ease. Help them feel that they are free to talk.
4   Remove distraction. Don't doodle, tap, shuffle papers or permit phone calls.
5   Empathize with the talker. Try to see their point of view and meet them halfway.
6   Be patient. Do not interrupt.
7   Watch out for emotionally charged words. Do not let them filter out the message.
8   Avoid personal prejudice. What the talker says, not how they look, is the important thing.
9   Listen to the tone in the talker's voice. Volume and tone can both be significant.
10   Watch for non-verbal communications. Gestures, facial expressions, body movements, eye-gaze direction and duration can all be important.

Alternatively, some organizations may choose to issue their employees with copies of the placard that appeared on the wall of former US president, Lyndon B Johnson; it read: 'You're not learning anything while you're talking.'

Without decrying the value of the list above, we must acknowledge that its value is limited. Effective listening requires practice. This also accounts for the limited success of packages that comprise a number of slides focusing on time spent listening and causes of ineffectiveness.

More successful training in effective listening involves course participants in role playing. Among the techniques most widely used is re-statement or paraphrasing. An emotionally charged subject is selected, and two persons with strongly conflicting views are required to discuss it. Each person speaks about ten times. The first, let us call them A, presents their arguments, then B has to paraphrase what was said. This paraphrasing must be to A's satisfaction before B is allowed to respond. The exchange continues for several iterations, each time following the same format. B and A soon learn to hear each other out and not register negative responses.

An observer logs the exchange as shown in Table 14.1.

Table 14.1 Paraphrasing

Complete	Accurate	Neither

The observer may spend ten minutes or thereabouts debriefing A and B.

A variant of re-statement or paraphrasing is summarizing. This differs in that it encompasses all the key points that have been made in the discussion up to each point of reply or response. It is not limited only to what was said in the last contribution by one of the participants. In any exchange a number of points may have been made. Hence summarizing can be important because it obliges each participant to sum up the other's central ideas together with supporting detail.

We can all take steps to improve our own listening. For example, we can listen to speakers on the radio, then try to work out the main theme from the digressions and supporting subject matter. Try to evaluate the argument. Notice any words that touch off your antagonism or arouse your sympathy. Note any appeals to prejudice, any statements that are cleverly worded to sound logical though they are not. Next try to re-state the gist of the talk for someone who did not hear it, or put it in an e-mail. Perhaps more of us should also try to listen more effectively when our spouse or partner talks. Not only would this be good practice for its own sake, but it might also improve family relations.

Returning our attention to work, we can expect a number of benefits if individuals listen more effectively. These include:

- A junior employee's hostile feelings may be markedly lessened if they are allowed to level with their senior, who hears them out.
- Better relationships may emerge if a manager becomes more sensitive to the feelings of their direct reports.
- Some genuine weakness in the organization may be brought into the open.

The effectiveness of listening training can be measured. One method is the Brown-Carlson test. This measures immediate recall: following directions, recognizing transitions, recognizing word meanings, and lecture comprehension. Before and after tests permit measurement of the progress made by the individual undertaking listening training. At the Pfizer company in the USA, sales personnel who had been given two-and-a-half hours' training in listening skills were tested after intervals of eight to ten weeks. The tests showed that good listening skills, once developed, are retained.

Other organizations have had similar experience. It appears that improved listening skills prove so useful that they are used continuously and perfected as a real result of constant practice.

It is relevant to make reference to the communication climate or overall atmosphere in which listening occurs. Generally communication climate is a result of the levels of trust, support and respect that exist among people in the organization. When there is a high level of trust and respect and a lack of fear, communication is much more open, honest and candid. Conversely, lack of respect for people's opinions and feelings results in a communication climate in which matters are filtered, with an impairment of effective listening in particular and communication in general.

Action plan

Irrespective of whether you have received training, the following is a useful personal action plan to sharpen up your listening effectiveness in preparation for an important meeting:

- List preoccupations most likely to distract you. What can be done to prevent them creating distraction? Resolve in advance that you will prevent your mind from drifting.
- Check for possible distractions and take the necessary steps to avoid or minimize them:
  - interruptions;
  - noise level;
  - general convenience/suitability of meeting place.
- Write down what you think is the other person's major objective that they hope to accomplish from the meeting, including any hidden agenda items.
- If you dislike or distrust the person with whom you must engage in conversation, list reasons for these feelings.

But note, you need to look beyond listening skills alone. A person may talk about one subject but really be concerned with another. Hence the effective listener has to learn to read the contours of the other person's thinking to find the hidden agenda. This is where skill in non-verbal communication is required.

15

Effective use of the telephone

Some people can't see a telephone without taking the receiver off.

W Somerset Maugham, *The Constant Wife*

In many cases the telephone is the front-line ambassador of an organization, which means that it must be answered promptly and in an effective manner. But the telephone can also be a great time waster and a source of interruptions.

When the leading US magazine *Fortune* asked more than 50 chairpersons, presidents and vice-presidents to rank the ten worst wasters of their valuable time, telephone interruptions headed the list. And the problem seems to be invading all levels of business life.

Hold that tiger

Some organizations have policies that encourage more efficient use of the telephone. For example, when the UK economy was in recession some years ago, as it is now, considerable savings were made in Ford UK by this means. However, two years later bad habits picked up again, so in a further attempt to improve telephone efficiency the company introduced TIGER equipment. This formidable acronym stood for Telephone Information Gathering for Evaluation and Review. A computer system logged all calls made and their length, and provided each department with data relating to their telephone use each month. Following its introduction in the UK headquarters, the net saving in expenditure on telephones was the not-inconsiderable amount of nine per cent in the first year.

Quiet hour

A smaller organization is unlikely to be able to afford such sophisticated equipment, but common-sense methods can still save considerable time and money. In some organizations top management agrees a 'quiet hour' each day between 9.30 and 10.30 am, for example, during which telephones will be kept silent as far as possible, with the service programmed accordingly to discourage any but top-priority calls. A further aid to its observance is to print details of the quiet period on stationery and business cards.

One company supports the practice with the following memo for external distribution:

> This is a reminder that our firm allows staff an uninterrupted morning work period from 8.30 to 10.00 am. If you try to reach us during those hours your call will be taken by a telephone answering system. Please leave your name and number if you'd like a call back. You can of course reach us directly at any time after 10.00 am. Thank you.

One of the gains for having a regular quiet period is that the rhythm of work is not disrupted, allowing goal-related tasks to be worked on without intrusion.

Cases where the quiet period is regularly abused internally should be treated as disciplinary matters and, if necessary, brought to the attention of senior management.

Evidence from surveys indicates that employees will respond to pressure and guidance about wasted telephone time.

Keeping a telephone log

Because a manager's time is rarely spent in the way they think it is, some objective analysis is necessary. The first step is to ascertain the gravity of the situation by keeping a simple log of incoming calls over a few days.

The minimum information required for this is the number of calls and the time it takes to deal with each one. If calls are routed through a direct report, this record can be kept by the direct report on behalf of the manager without demanding any of the latter's own time. The results of this initial record will help to determine whether a more detailed analysis is necessary to trace the source of the calls: whether they are mainly internal or external. Each of these categories can then be subjected to further study.

For internal calls it may be necessary to know:

- the department initiating the call;
- whether it comes from the boss, a peer, a team member or a direct report;
- the timing and duration of each call;
- the reason for each call;
- whether it was justified, either at all or when compared with other possible methods of communication.

External calls may need separate analysis, for which a possible layout is given in Figure 15.1. This covers both incoming and outgoing calls.

A card like this can be filled in each time the telephone is used during the period of the survey. Periodically, the cards can be analysed and the findings used as the basis for remedial action.

Name of manager	Date
Name of other party	Subject
Direction of call: inbound/outbound	
Subject	Duration
Assessed value of call: high/medium/low (my priority rating)	
Justification or comment	

Figure 15.1 Telephone analysis card

The comment section may be used for notes relating to how the call could have been avoided, eg by sending an e-mail.

Make a habit of periodically checking the duration of phone calls. Some managers have digital clocks on their desks that become electronic timers at the press of a button. Alternatively, an hourglass or a glance at a watch can provide an approximate idea of the duration of a call. Bad habits develop and periodic time checks indicate whether action is required. By setting yourself a limit for the duration of the phone call you can save a lot of time.

In using such an analysis to avoid wasted time, consider factors such as:

- personal preferences and habits;
- levels of confidentiality of information;
- location of phone in relation to colleagues nearby;
- cultural factors, eg a preference for this form of communication among certain groups.

Ways to communicate without using a telephone include fax and e-mail. Both override global time zones.

Video conferencing is another option. Its main pros and cons include:

Pros:
- saves time and money on travel;
- enables building of 'virtual' teams and organizations by bringing together people who may be widely dispersed.

Cons:
- although costs have fallen, it can still be expensive;
- opportunities for human contact are reduced.

With the acceptance of internet protocol (IP) telecom services, new products are emerging that use the desktop computer.

Effective screening by a PA

Those who have a PA must ensure that they have clear instructions regarding:

- which calls the manager will take;
- whether to interrupt the manager;
- whether to transfer the call if the manager is in a colleague's office;
- which calls the manager's colleagues will handle.

With careful prompting, many outside callers will be willing to disclose to a PA details of the subject they wish to discuss with the manager. This often happens where the PA says, 'I am afraid X is on the other line at the moment but if you could tell me the nature of your call I will get the necessary information and have it ready for when they return your call.'

Another technique is for the manager to arrange to be officially 'away from the office' for the morning and have their PA collate incoming calls during this period so that they can be dealt with en bloc that afternoon on the manager's 'return'.

In the absence of a PA, it may be possible to arrange for a colleague to answer all calls during certain hours. Arrangements of this nature ensure that each person can have some protected time.

Use the telephone effectively

To deal more effectively with the telephone, the prime need is to develop better working habits. Often where two managers in the same office face very similar problems of excessive time spent on the telephone, it will be found that one or the other is markedly more efficient in coping. This may well reflect differences in personality, but in addition the less efficient of the two may have the following traits:

- is unable to resist a ringing bell;
- uses the phone for socializing;
- feels indispensable and answers all calls personally;
- overrates self-importance when dealing with others;
- has a compulsive urge to be involved;
- feels insecure when others handle calls;
- lacks ability to end conversations politely and quickly;
- cannot assess time being spent on a call;
- has failed to train their PA to screen incoming calls;
- fails to anticipate information required and have it at hand when calls are expected.

Methods that will improve effectiveness on the phone include:

- Encourage managers to think before picking up the phone to make an outgoing call and to consider whether it is the best use of their time. If so, the message should be tailored to suit the recipient and delivered as expeditiously as possible.
- Concentrate, for without any eye contact you can easily be distracted by, for example, the paper on your desk.
- Limit social conversation. Without seeming discourteous, only the matter in hand should be dealt with.
- Points should be made succinctly.
- Use the primacy and recency effects: people recall most easily the things heard first and last. So start with a summary of the points to be made, spell these out in greater detail and conclude with a brief review of them.
- Before making a call, think if the timing is right. Phoning just before lunch or at the end of the working day is the ideal time for dealing with verbose people.

If the line is bad, hang up and call back.

Use the type of phone and service best suited to your needs

Telephones have a vast range of optional extras and services. In the UK, for example, BT offers:

Call waiting: know when someone's trying to get through;
Call diversion: diverts to another phone;
Call sign: additional number with a different ring tone;
Ring back: know when an engaged number is free;
Reminder call: book an alarm call;
Three-way calling: allows three callers to talk together;
Caller display: see who's calling;
Call barring: bar certain outgoing calls;
Dial 1471: know the last caller;
1471 extra: know the last five callers;
Internet call waiting: alerts you if someone calls you while BT communicator is running online and line is engaged;
Internet call barring: stops certain types of calls being made with BT communicator while online.

Choose a system with the features you actually need, as there is no point in having features you will not use.

A telephone equipped with an electronic memory or an automatic redial can be useful. But be careful if you are making a highly confidential call. You should then consider dialling a different number so that the confidential number is not left in the phone's memory.

A telephone amplifier or cordless phone may be desirable. It enables callers to allow another party who is in the office to hear the conversation, or to keep the conversation going while you extract the relevant file or have your hands free to make notes.

Also available is a voice messenger – a form of voicemail that not only enables callers to leave messages but also allows them to record and transmit an identical message simultaneously to anyone possessing a mailbox within the system. Recipients do not need to be available when the message is sent. This avoids having to phone several people with the same information. Each country's telephone service will have its own array of optional extras.

Some time-saving tips

Prepare your calls in advance. For example:

■ If you have a PA, ask them to phone and ascertain if the other party is ready to take your call; the PA can also enquire if the other party has any points they wish to raise that the direct report can deal with before transferring the call to you.
■ If the person to whom you wish to speak is not available, leave a message with their direct report to arrange a convenient call-back time:
  – know the points to be made;
  – have to hand any necessary files or papers;
  – have regard to telephone charges.
■ When you have to make a number of calls:
  – organize them in order of priority;
  – consider the schedules of the people you are contacting and ensure you don't make unnecessary calls;
  – try to reserve a particular time of the day to make the calls.
■ Ensure that you have the telephone numbers readily available. Time spent finding numbers can often be avoided by using a memory telephone, which stores a list of numbers and has single-button facilities to redial engaged numbers. Other ways of keeping numbers to hand are:
  – a card that you can carry in a pocket;
  – a card index on your desk;
  – your PC.
■ If you are asked to hold, you may:
  – decline to be put on hold and ask when it would be convenient to call back;

- ask to leave a message, particularly if you have already been asked three or four times to hold;
- wait, in which case have a magazine, report, or something to hand that can gainfully employ your time. Only do this if the other party is extremely difficult to contact or if you wish to avoid hanging up and wasting the call.

■ While away from your desk, ensure you have your mobile phone and that it is adequately charged. This can help to reduce tension and allows you to make productive use of travelling time. However, you must ensure that:
- you do not infringe any traffic law relating to driving and phoning;
- you do not annoy other people;
- you do not give away confidential information to others who may overhear you;
- the use of the phone does not become an addiction.

■ As a rule, mobile phones should be turned off before a meeting. If you are expecting a call that you must take, warn the person you are meeting beforehand and leave the room to take the call.

■ Telephone credit cards: although more expensive, these can be extremely useful if it is necessary to make a long-distance call from a friend's home telephone without loading their bill. The card has the added advantage of providing a printed record of all calls for which it has been used.

Taking phone calls

Receiving phone calls is very different from making them. Incoming calls can interrupt you or take you by surprise, so develop techniques to handle them. Ways of doing this include:

■ Tell people the times when you are available to take calls;
■ Make your first question, 'How long is this call likely to take?' Depending on the answer, you may decide to ask the person to call back at a time to suit your convenience;

■ Treat cold callers courteously but firmly – they are only doing their job.

When terminating a call, be polite, be firm – and be gone.

Devise some polite but ruthless methods for ending calls. For example, pre-arrange with your PA for an imaginary visitor to arrive at the appointed time then turn to your 'visitor' and say, 'Sorry to keep you waiting, I'm just finishing this call,' in such a way that the person at the other end of the line is bound to hear and will hopefully take the hint.

An exception to this may be necessary, however, depending on the caller. For example, if they are a major client, then taking the call may be advisable no matter how inconvenient the time.

Make notes

It often pays to make a brief note of what was said during important phone calls. This may appear tedious but can save a lot of time in wrangling afterwards about what was said, or trying to remember what was agreed.

Make the notes during the call. Phones have a habit of ringing again immediately after a call has finished. Keep all your notes in one place unless there is a specific file for the information.

Save the time of others

The phone should be answered within three rings. Clear procedures should exist and be followed for taking and passing on messages. For example, you should give your name, and sound warm, welcoming and smiling. The caller cannot see you but will quickly form an impression of you. If you smile, it will convey in the tone of your voice that you are friendly and approachable. Likewise, be enthusiastic.

If you promise to return the call, you should do so promptly. In the event you are unable to do so, you should brief the person who has to return the call.

In short, the manner in which phone calls are handled depends in no small measure on a manager's self-concept and assertiveness, and on the importance they attach to their own time conservation. This must be weighed against the perceived importance of the time they are prepared to spend on the telephone. The development of effective working habits is also important.

Finally, if you insist that you must answer all external calls personally because the callers are too important to be handled by someone else, remind yourself that the organization you work for still functions satisfactorily during your annual vacation periods.

16

Effective use of technology

The privileged in today's world are the un-wired.

Anonymous

Developments in communications technology offer businesses a multitude of new ways in which to communicate and pass information back and forth. Yet whereas many of these technologies can offer obvious advantages in efficiency to businesses competing in today's markets, it is worth noting that as well as the many blessings they offer, many of them can also prove to be a curse.

Of all the electronic technologies, e-mail has become by far the most widespread and integrated communications medium since the telephone, and it is for that reason that its effects on modern business must be examined in more detail.

Few businesses could exist without e-mail – it is accepted both as a means of informal communication, similar to the way in which we use the telephone, and also as a formal medium for recording conversations and decisions, much like the traditional letter.

Essentially e-mail can facilitate:

- ease of communication wherever people are located or based;
- swift transfer of all requisite information;
- speedy communication to all concerned once a decision has been made.

However, unless managed effectively, e-mail can become extremely time consuming, to the point where simply 'keeping the ball rolling' can become a job in itself. Indeed, it would be fair to say that the advantages brought about in speed and ease of communication are countered by the increase in the volume of e-mail received, and those who most complain about e-mails are probably the same people who previously complained about the number of memos received and the ever-ringing phone.

Furthermore, developments in the ways in which these new forms of electronic information are received have also taken place. No longer is work confined to the workplace. Instead, to make our lives 'easier' the office now moves – constantly. Communication by e-mail or telephone may be done at home, on the train, on the plane or even on vacation. But is this necessarily a good thing? While people are freed from the daily commute to work this 'always available' technology may lead to a feeling of never really being off duty.

E-mail now means that outsiders can access you, although if you have a PA, that person can still remain the gatekeeper and deal with the messages. To ensure this:

- brief your PA;
- involve your PA;
- delegate to the lowest possible level.

A clearly defined system must be in place that will ensure that only one of you replies and the e-mail is handled only by one person.

E-mail brings with it many problems such as receiving junk e-mail, dealing with e-mail 'commandos', receiving unnecessary copies and so on, which can lead to information overload. It is a case of the classic problem in which the urgent drives out the important. It sometimes takes so long to get through all the junk that when people get to the important messages it may be too late to act. Further, people sending e-mail assume that the recipient checks their e-mails regularly and will act on them.

Because of their immediacy and ease of use, e-mail and other electronic means of communication are 'faceless' when compared to meetings, handwritten letters and, to a lesser degree, the telephone. Hence, according to social scientists, there is a greater risk of 'faceless strangers' running into problems. For example, because certain important communication aspects are missing in e-mail – facial expressions, gestures, tone of voice, etc, the absence of everyday pleasantries can make a message come across as rude. And given that first impressions often set the tone for subsequent interaction, things can rapidly deteriorate. So, according to some psychologists, talking first on the phone, for example, might set expectations at a more appropriate level – an effect that can then continue into an e-mail relationship.

Other problems that e-mail can cause include:

- Employer's liability. E-mails sent by employees in the course of their employment are the responsibility of the employer. The employer is liable in law for the actions of the employee even if the employee was disobeying company rules and regulations. Disclaimers should be included in all e-mails sent by or on behalf of the employer.
- Lack of confidentiality. Even though an e-mail is electronic and can be deleted, it could have been printed first; and even if it has been deleted and not printed, it is in fact still recoverable on the computer.
- The 'squirrel syndrome' applies to e-mail just as it does to ordinary mail and can lead to unwieldy mailboxes, making information hard to find and taking up valuable disk space.
- Because e-mail is commonly used for informal as well as formal messaging, people are prone to putting things in e-mail they would never say in person, and this may return to haunt them later.
- E-mail can easily be sent to the wrong address by a simple wrong click or keystroke, and may provide unintended opportunities to the competition.
- E-mails are the most common form of transferring viruses and other harmful programs that can damage your computer and your company's data.

A system for e-mail

Previously communications in the workplace were mostly point-to-point, meaning that only messages that were intended specifically for the recipient were received. Now, with the ability to broadcast to many recipients at once by e-mail, recipients have to spend time dealing with many irrelevant e-mails. So it is vital to have a well-defined system in place to deal with your e-mails effectively. Most important, your system should address how many of your e-mails are of no interest or no importance (including spam) and what steps can be taken to eliminate their receipt in future.

Furthermore, your system should also take into account your work methods, the way you prioritize, how you prefer to communicate, how you like to delegate and which part of the day is the best for handling e-mails. The system developed will most likely be applicable to a wider audience, ie to your team and possibly to the whole organization. For instance, have clear guidelines been established regarding the use of e-mail? If so, is everyone complying?

Although most companies base their e-mail policies around the nature of the organization and to what extent it is dependent on e-mail as a means of doing business, it is worth noting that some have established policies such as allowing employees to access their e-mail twice a day – after arrival in the morning and after lunch. This kind of batching is the fastest way to minimize time lost on social communication. Another policy is to ban staff from communicating internally via e-mail, although some organizations, such as Microsoft, have encouraged a culture based on e-mail rather than the telephone, as it results in fewer interruptions.

It is also worth noting that the culture of the organization can influence the number of e-mails sent. High levels of copied and stored e-mails may be indicative of an organization where back-covering is prevalent because of a blame culture. Likewise, e-mails from persons at home or on vacation may, on the one hand, indicate an extremely committed and highly work-conscious individual or, on the other hand, a high level of fear or paranoia within the organization.

It is also vitally important that your computer, your office network and your data are secure, well-managed and protected against electronic threat.

This is particularly the case where e-mail is concerned, because no other medium is as dangerous in transferring malicious software that can damage and disrupt communications systems and destroy data. Malicious software, or 'malware' as it is collectively known, includes common threats such as viruses, trojans, worms and spyware.

It is therefore vital that organizations – and, indeed, home users – incorporate technology such as firewalls, e-mail and internet web filters, anti-virus, anti-spam and anti-spyware software to prevent the misuse of this technology.

Responding to e-mail

It is essential that management educate and train their workforce in responding to e-mails. Training or guidance on this may come from organizational policies, but where this is not forthcoming or people are self-employed, the following guidelines may prove helpful:

- Junk it if not relevant by deleting it. Delegate it if appropriate. Otherwise *do it*.
- Act and respond on the first reading. Otherwise put it in your 'must do' folder.
- If you cannot respond fully at the moment, send a brief, but not terse, response.
- Cover only one topic per e-mail. It's then easier for the reader to take action on it.
- Put the message in context and ensure that the subject matter on the subject line is clearly stated.

- If the topic has changed, change the subject line to reflect more accurately the new content.
- Make priorities clear. If you expect action, specify from whom and by when.
- Kept messages should be filed properly and stored in the correct files if printed out. Print only if necessary.
- Write as a reporter writes a news article: use short paragraphs and deliver the key facts first.
- If revising or adding text, use a different font type or colour so that it is obvious to the recipient.
- Try not to compose a message when angry and don't write in capitals (e-mail 'shouting').
- It is difficult to express tone, mood or body language in e-mail; exercise care with humour.
- Remember that e-mail is less effective for decisions of a more personal or emotional nature.
- Beware snappy e-mails; one person's efficiency can be interpreted as rudeness by another.
- Always spellcheck your e-mail.

Voicemail

Voicemail technology has greatly improved in recent years, taking it far beyond that of the simple answering machine. It has a number of advantages including:

- It can be an effective cost cutter. It may do away with the need to employ receptionists.
- Fellow employees are not disturbed by a colleague's continually ringing phone.
- If you have switched on your voicemail because you are busy, an incoming message can be heard as it is recorded and dealt with personally if of sufficient importance and urgency.
- By switching off your phone and letting people leave a message, you can phone back at your convenience while at the same time batching calls. That way you can control the conversation and save time.

- You can have a system that ranks and filters telephone calls. For example, when the CEO calls, their message, flagged by the incoming number, can be placed at the top of the list of calls to make.
- Messages can be left when the person called is not available. This can be particularly useful to certain groups of people, eg those working from home or without a direct report.
- As we mentioned in Chapter 15, voice messengers enable callers to leave messages and allow them to record and transmit an identical message simultaneously to anyone possessing a mailbox within the system. Recipients do not need to be available when the message is sent. This avoids having to ring several people with the same information.
- Voicemail can be operated by remote control so that messages can be taken even when you are not in your office or at home. For example, during absences overseas, if there is no one back at base to take calls, in many countries you can programme your home or office phone to divert incoming calls automatically to the number where you are located.
- If you phone someone anticipate voicemail and have your message ready. This may spare the listener from a rambling disorganized message.
- Research has shown that you almost double your chance of getting a return call if you use voicemail instead of e-mail. The voice seems to contain a greater sense of urgency than text on a screen.

When recording a voicemail message:

- be brief, crisp and speak slowly, as if you were speaking to someone who speaks your language as a second language;
- on your home phone do not give your name: using your number instead lets genuine callers know if they dialled correctly but does not tell crank callers and potential burglars whose home they have reached.

In a growing number of organizations, teams have replaced departments as the basic unit. They can be permanent or assembled for particular tasks. They can be in close proximity, including sharing an office, or widely dispersed geographically. The teams, however, are generally held together by high-tech communication systems, such as computerized diaries, e-mail, voicemail, mobile phones and faxes. But for many people, voicemail ranks third on business-related hate lists, after traffic wardens and junk mail. A variety of factors contribute to this:

- Voicemail can cause a great deal of stress if the systems have been set up by IT specialists who do not understand how teams operate. Team secretaries are better equipped to set up user-friendly voicemail systems.
- There is a loss of intimacy. A person can hide behind the voicemail.
- The voicemail system is poorly set up. This can be avoided as follows:
  - The message should say who you are and what you do.
  - The message should repeat any numbers and avoid time wasters such as 'Have a nice day.'
  - The bleep should occur immediately after your message is finished.
  - Try to leave the number of an available co-worker.
  - Regularly update your greeting message. For example, do not leave the message, 'Just away from my desk,' when you are taking a week's leave, or 'Today, March...' when it is April.

Social impact

The widespread use of portable communications devices and methods has created a downside for nomadic employees, namely the development of a 'corporate presence'. Your boss, colleagues and others are able to detect whether you are logged into the organization's network, be it at home, in the office or out on the move. This has huge implications for your work–life balance, privacy and stress.

Further, remote working reduces social networking, a factor that can really drive performance. To combat this, organizations must allocate resources to allow personal meetings and events that will reinforce social networks. Only where strong social networks exist can technology strengthen and nurture them.

17

Dealing with a boss who wastes your time

> I call the shots around here and if you don't like it, you know what you can do!
>
> Hyam T Guvnor (well-known boss of the 'old school')

Does the mere mention of the word 'boss' produce strong emotions in you? Do you have the kind of boss who talks like the one quoted above?

Much of what is written about time management assumes a situation in which you are in control. For many people this is not the case. When you are a direct report you cannot by definition make the rules, except for some very minor ones concerning only yourself and those who report to you.

So there are no simple and infallible rules for dealing with a boss who persists in wasting your time and possibly also their own. Any improvement can occur only as the result of increasing your boss's awareness of the problem, plus a long-term programme of 'boss education'. If you are not prepared to engage in this, then there would appear to be only three alternatives:

Try to negotiate by providing straightforward input to the boss as to how their habits result in you being less effective.
Resign or seek a transfer.
Learn to live with the unsatisfactory situation – and possibly cope with the ensuing ulcers and other stress symptoms that this may give you.

But do not despair; given patience and determination, it is possible not only to learn to manage your boss's present unsatisfactory behaviour but also to help them decide whether it is in both your interests for them to change their behaviour towards you. This chapter offers a number of ways for dealing practically with the situation.

Attitudes towards the boss

In many organizations, boss–direct report relationships leave much to be desired, and this can have vast consequences in terms of time wasting and general ineffectiveness.

At one extreme the boss may be seen as an institutional enemy who is permanently wrong and held to blame for all evils and mistakes that occur. Where this is so, behaviour patterns develop that psychologists describe as counter-dependency: it becomes natural to rebel against the boss or any other authority figure simply for the sake of being controversial.

At the other extreme are those who see their boss as completely infallible and either through fear or uncritical admiration never venture any disagreement or adverse opinion. Psychologists call this over-dependency. The most serious consequences of this include producing a mass of 'yes-people', a serious lack of personal development and a moribund organization where work comes to a standstill whenever a minor decision has to be made and there is no boss around to make it.

Between these two ghastly extremes there is plenty of middle ground to be explored, and we are aiming to help you use the same skills in exploring and managing your attitude to your boss that you would naturally apply to any other person or situation without being overawed by the gap in authority between you.

Who is at fault?

If you have worked for the same boss for a long time, always remember that, perhaps unwittingly, you may have 'trained' them to waste your time. For instance, there may have been occasions when you made yourself too available or too ready to take on tasks that were really those of the boss or other colleagues. Or you may have failed to delegate some tasks to your own direct reports in the mistaken belief that the boss prefers it that way. These actions may have set up a situation in which your boss perceives you as having an inexhaustible need for more work. This has caused them to undervalue your time. This can usually be corrected by being more open with your boss about your current workload and by getting them to let you know the current priorities of the various jobs you have in hand at any time.

You may also have confused respect with deference, particularly with a strong boss.

Yet such people do not have respect for complainers. You do not have to be defensive. Constructive challenge can create a better working relationship. When trying this, do not rush what you are saying, and remember the importance of verbal communication. Presentation can be more important than content.

Believing is not always seeing

Sometimes the boss's behaviour may appear to you to be wasting your time. In making such a judgement, however, do recognize that you may not have accurate or full information as to why your boss has behaved in such a fashion. For instance, your boss may know better than you what the organization requires of you both. Nor are some executives wildly communicative on the subject of plans and priorities. Further, these demands can change at short notice. Hence, it is always advantageous as a starting point to try to understand your boss's organizational and personal objectives. This can be helped in part by observing how your boss behaves when in action with their superiors.

Likewise, it is essential to become aware of your boss's own work style. For instance, how does your boss prefer to receive information from other sources? In terms of Peter Drucker's classification, is your boss mainly a 'listener' or a 'reader'? If the former, brief your boss in person; if the latter let your boss have an e-mail.

Helping the work flow

Whenever a work assignment is under consideration between you, always seek to obtain answers from the boss at the briefing stage to such questions as What? When? Where? How? Why? before accepting it. This will help to avoid interruptions later. Likewise, when preparing to report back with the results, always try to anticipate the questions under these same headings that the boss will quite probably ask in order to understand and clarify what you have delivered.

When a boss appears to vacillate, it is important not to strain your mutual relationship by pressing too hard for a quick decision; it is better to ask, 'When can I call back for an answer to this one?' than to risk annoyance by insisting on an instant answer.

Giving the boss effective response

Never undervalue the use of effective response when trying to improve a relationship, even if it is the boss to whom you are talking. In practice, many direct reports complain about their boss without first seeking to improve the situation by giving feedback. For example, the direct report may complain that the boss never listens. When this appears to be the case, a good way to tackle it is to attempt to provide some genuine response by proceeding as follows:

- Select with care a time in which to share this impression with the boss, avoiding occasions when the boss is clearly 'on the run'.
- Make your point succinctly, indicating how this information can benefit the boss and your mutual relationship.
- Try to get a reaction from the boss by interspersing these remarks with questions such as, 'How do you feel about that?'
- If the boss indicates a desire to think over what you have said before giving a reaction, try to agree a date for a further

meeting on the matter and offer to send a short confirmatory e-mail.

■ If the boss interrupts you a great deal, find a suitable moment to explain how (perhaps after reading this book!) you are seeking to improve your time management in both your own and the organization's interests and that perhaps you could draw up between you a reporting schedule so as to minimize interruptions to the work of your department.

■ Learn to manage the boss's expectations. One way to achieve this is by down-playing the boss's expectations.

If a deadline is going to be missed, the boss may be angry. But if the boss thinks the deadline will be missed by five days and you know you may be able to get this down to two days and you deliver on that, the boss is more likely to be pleased with you.

Managing your relationship with the boss

Ways to achieve this include:

■ information transfer, ie telling the boss more of what you know or feel;

■ focusing on one or two relevant areas of behaviour with which to influence the boss, eg listening versus interrupting;

■ taking the lead by asking questions and exploring ideas with the boss;

■ identifying any weaknesses that the boss may have, and trying to compensate for these;

■ behaviour modelling: setting a good example by the way you handle your own work, your time and your direct reports;

■ appealing to an outside authority, eg a mutual contact who is on good terms with both of you and can plant a suitable word in the boss's ear at an appropriate time.

Professors John Gabarro and John Kotter offer some general advice in this area:

- Make every effort to understand your boss's job, personal style and context including their:
  - goals and objectives;
  - work-related pressures;
  - strengths, weaknesses and blind spots;
  - preferred working style.
- Assess yourself and your own needs including your:
  - strengths and weaknesses;
  - predisposition towards authority and dependence;
  - personal working style;
  - preferred style for the boss to work with you.
- Try to develop and maintain a relationship that:
  - fits the needs of both you and your boss;
  - is based on dependability and honesty;
  - is characterized by mutual expectations;
  - keeps the boss informed;
  - selectively makes the best use of your boss's time and resources.

Upward delegation

Another strategy is to resort to upward delegation. Donald Wass and William Oncken neatly illustrate the manner in which a partially finished job may be shuffled onto the boss:

> Let us imagine that a manager is walking down the hall and that he notices one of his subordinates, A, coming up the hallway. When they are abreast of one another, A greets the manager with 'Good morning. By the way, we've got a problem. You see...'. As A continues, the manager recognizes in this problem the same two characteristics common to all the problems his subordinates gratuitously bring to his attention: the manager knows enough to get involved but not enough to make the on-the-spot decision expected of him. Eventually the manager says, 'So glad you brought this up. I'm in a rush right now. Meanwhile, let me think about it and I'll let you know.' Then he and A part company.

Before the two of them met, whose back was the monkey on? The subordinate's. After they parted, whose back was it on? The manager's. Subordinate-imposed time begins the moment a monkey successfully executes a leap from the back of a subordinate to the back of the manager, and it does not end until the monkey is returned to its proper owner for care and feeding.

It's in your own interest

It isn't absolutely necessary to like or even admire the person for whom you work; but it helps if you do. The important thing is to manage the relationship between you. If you cannot do this jointly, it is worth working on it unilaterally despite the gap in authority. Your boss is one of the main resources for your personal achievement and advancement. Certainly a prescription for your own future success is to work for a boss who is going places. Only frustration and failure are on the horizon for you if you have an incompetent boss and make no attempt to do anything about it. It is much better to support and educate such a person than to spend your time criticizing and seeking to undermine the person who holds all the best cards.

Concluding comment

It can also be a salutary experience to ask other people, 'What do I do that takes your time without contributing to your effectiveness?'

18

Effective delegation

Here lies John, who said last year, 'I cannot delegate, my dear.'
Too late the doctor's diagnosis: acute non-delegos thrombosis.
Poor John, he had a staff of nine, yet wouldn't pass work down
the line,
    Preferred to take a bagful home; his widow struggles on
alone.

Anonymous

Delegation is one of the most effective methods of liberating time. It consists of giving a task to another person to complete on your behalf. You give the person the responsibility for completing the task and you provide the commensurate authority. In other words, you delegate authority and responsibility. You cannot delegate accountability, as you remain accountable to your boss for the work carried out by your direct reports. This is depicted in Figure 18.1.

Advantages of delegation

There are many advantages of delegation, to both managers and their employees. First, for the manager effective delegation results in higher productivity as it provides more time. Second, the manager gains more respect from their employees. Third, the workflow speeds up by reducing or eliminating bottlenecks such as approval or signature for routine decisions. Fourth, employees are being developed, and this helps ensure trained replacements. In fact, part of a manager's job is the development of direct reports. And fifth, by having more highly trained replacements you increase your chances for promotion.

    The advantages to the employee are numerous. Productivity increases through higher motivation. Research has repeatedly shown that employees seek responsibility, challenge, variety,

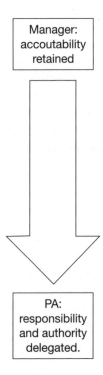

Figure 18.1 Delegation of responsibility and authority

professional growth, experience and authority in their jobs. Delegation provides these factors with the accompanying motivation.

Although delegation can be a great time saver, there is a catch-22: until you have trained the people to whom you wish to delegate, you are not in a position to do so. But training takes time and, like most of life's situations, it requires an initial investment of time.

Types of delegation

When we think of delegation, we normally think of downward delegation. This is the traditional type of delegation, where you give work to people who report directly to you. One of the basic principles of organizations is that you delegate to the lowest level possible commensurate with ability. However, there is also horizontal delegation, which is delegation to another who is at the same level as yourself in the organizational hierarchy. It may be delegation to a team member, in which case it is known as delegation by consensus or consensual delegation. It could also be delegation to a person in another department. This is known as delegation by persuasion. It may be a project or an assignment that is particularly interesting to an individual in another department, and that person may be willing to be involved for professional development purposes.

The third type of delegation is upward delegation. As we saw in Chapter 17, we can think of this as the 'monkey on your back' syndrome: a direct report gives the manager something they themselves should be doing or returns some work that remains incomplete. The employee may say something like 'I've been working on this for over two hours and I'm not getting anywhere. I know you could get it done in a few minutes, so if I leave it with you I'll be able to get on with the rest of the work I'm doing for you.' If you allow this to happen, you will suffer the consequences. These are twofold. First, you have reinforced the type of behaviour you should be trying to discourage, ie upward or reverse delegation; and second, you are wasting your time.

There are two golden rules for preventing improper upward delegation:

1 Accept unfinished work from direct reports only in exceptional circumstances; problems may be brought for discussion and should be accompanied by suggested solutions. You may counsel, advise and encourage but must ensure that the delegated authority remains fairly and squarely with the person who accepted it.
2 Limit your own involvement by the clock; failure to do so will merely encourage your direct reports to bring you more problems.

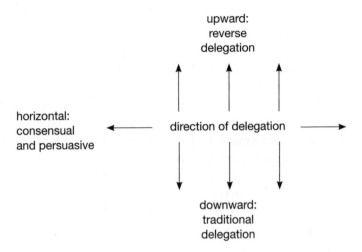

Figure 18.2 Types of delegation

Why managers don't delegate

For delegation to take place, you need three things:

something that you can delegate;
someone to whom you can delegate;
a willingness to delegate.

The rest is up to you. However, we know that most managers do not delegate as much as they could. Let's look at some of the reasons.

Many managers don't delegate because they feel that if they do, the task won't be done in the same way they would do it. Others feel the task won't be done as well as they could do it themselves. Both views may well be right. However, the question these managers should be asking is, 'Will it be done in a manner acceptable to the organization?' If so, the task should be delegated.

Closely aligned to this is the problem of perfection. When Peters and Waterman wrote their bestseller, they called it *In Search of Excellence*, not *In Search of Perfection*. Excellence should be a goal in every organization. The quest for perfection is time wasting, frustrating and stress inducing. Have you ever met a happy perfectionist?

Some managers merely lack the knowledge. Delegation is a management skill that can be learnt. Without this skill it is impossible to delegate effectively. If a manager lacks the appropriate skill to do something, they will avoid the task. It is human nature to avoid doing something that would show up our inefficiency. Performance appraisal and disciplining are other examples of this type of task: people avoid them if they do not have the necessary training to do them effectively.

Some managers are inhibited about delegation because of a fear of employees' reactions. They fear that the employees will be thinking they are being dumped on. These employees are the same ones that say 'Goodnight' to their managers as they leave the office at 5 pm while their managers are there until 7 or 8 pm. This fear is particularly acute with newly appointed managers. These managers need to remind themselves that the definition of management is 'achieving objectives through and with others'.

Some managers don't delegate because they believe that it would take longer to delegate the job than to do it themselves. This may be true. However, if the task is of a recurring nature, then the initial investment of time in training someone to do it will reap enormous benefits, as it will no longer have to be done by the manager.

Another reason is that some managers' desire for personal credit supersedes their willingness to delegate a high-profile task. This is rather unfortunate and alienating for the direct report.

There are some managers who prefer to do certain tasks themselves, even though these tasks could and should be delegated. If the task could be delegated and is not, this leads to ineffective management. While working in the insurance business in Montreal some years ago, one of the authors of this book observed that a trip to Bermuda was necessary to finalize marine policy renewals at the end of March each year. While this trip could have been taken by any of the managers in the marine department, the president of the company himself always made the trip. Anyone familiar with the climates of Montreal and Bermuda will realize how attractive a trip to Bermuda is at the end of March. It's a wonderful transition from snow and skiing to sun and surfing. This president also happened to be an enthusiastic golfer. This is an example of something that could and should have been delegated.

Why isn't delegation done more often?

A manager who fails to delegate is not really managing effectively. The following are some further reasons why managers don't delegate:

- lack of confidence in the ability of direct reports;
- belief that they will be blamed by their boss if inappropriate decisions are taken by direct reports;
- fear of direct reports outclassing them or moving ahead too fast;
- belief in their own indispensability;
- fear of not getting the credit for good decisions taken on their behalf;
- desire to make the job more complicated than it really is;
- fear of losing control, status or job security;
- lack of trust in staff;
- unwillingness to take risks;
- reluctance to give up an enjoyable job or one they do particularly well;
- lack of willingness or ability to direct the efforts of others or involve them;
- feeling more comfortable handling detail than managing people.

What are the indicators of a poor delegator?

In many cases there is an underlying inertia that inhibits delegation. Many people find it less troublesome to keep everything under personal control than let it out of sight. A conscious and deliberate effort is needed to get out of such an attitude, and those who fail to do so can often be readily identified by a number of warning signs, such as:

- the number of interruptions in the working day;
- the boss regularly working longer hours than their direct reports;
- carrying a heavy briefcase of work home night after night;
- having a continually full in-basket and pending tray;
- having a backlog of e-mails;
- having a desk covered with papers;
- constant rushing to meet deadlines, and appearing under constant pressure or stress;
- insufficient time to discuss matters with staff or colleagues;
- direct reports constantly having to seek approval before they can take any action.

As regards the oft-heard phrase, 'But there is no one to whom I can delegate,' the answer is, 'You'd better hurry up and develop someone; if not, it reflects on you!'

To obtain an indication of your own present effectiveness as a delegator, try completing the checklist in Figure 18.3.

After completing the checklist, study the delegation profile that emerges. If your answers are honest, you will almost inevitably find that you should delegate more and/or better than you do at present.

How to delegate

The process by which work is delegated is a critical interface between manager and direct report. Inadequate delegation of work can result in:

- misdirected effort;
- confusion around priorities;
- waste of time;
- waste of money;

- waste of energy;
- waste of resources;
- conflict;
- stress.

	Never	Sometimes	Often
Do you take work home: – at nights? – at weekends?			
Do you work longer hours than: – your boss? – your peers? – your direct reports?			
Are you heavily backlogged with work when you have been away for: – a day? – a week? – a holiday?			
Do you face constant pressure to meet deadlines?			
Do you delegate only when there is a high proportion of urgent tasks?			
Do you delegate jobs you enjoy doing?			
Do you develop your staff by: – training them? – coaching them? – giving them guidance?			
When delegating do you: – pass complete tasks to direct reports? – give them complete authority? – define the task clearly but not rigidly?			
Do you check on direct reports after delegating tasks to them?			

Figure 18.3 Delegation checklist

The steps involved in delegating effectively are:

1 Determine what to delegate. The first step in this is to have a close look at your job description. You will realize that there are certain tasks you cannot delegate, such as hiring, firing, conducting performance appraisals, handling grievances, disciplining, coaching, counselling, scheduling the work of direct reports, preparing your department's budget, making salary decisions, proposing promotions, handling certain highly sensitive, personal, confidential, political or security issues, etc. Tasks such as routine activities, clerical duties such as filing, counting, sorting, record keeping, completing forms, sending faxes, preparing routine reports such as monthly attendance records, and much research (internet and other) should be delegated. Many phone calls and e-mails can also be delegated. By delegating whole jobs rather than pieces you build a sense of commitment and get better results.

   The following are factors to take into consideration when deciding what to delegate:

   decisions you make most often;
   functions that make you over-specialized;
   areas in which direct reports need development;
   things that will add variety and challenge to direct reports' jobs;
   areas in which your staff are better qualified than you;
   responsibilities from your last job assignment;
   tasks that do not directly meet your job objectives.

   More and more managers are being asked to make sophistic-ated presentations these days. One of the authors recently visited a Fortune 500 company and was told that all managers are expected to do all their own typing and preparation of their PowerPoint presentations. Such preparation can take managers many hours. The same work could be completed in a fraction of the time by a competent PA. Managers are supposed to manage, not do clerical work. Again we go back to the organizational principle: delegate to the lowest level possible commensurate with ability.

2 Determine the end result. Prior to delegating to a direct report or team member, the manager must be clear in their own mind what they expect, when they want the job done and how much effort they want their direct report or team member to put into the assignment they are delegating.

3 Determine to whom the task will be given. This is decided by the abilities, knowledge and skills of the direct report or team member, their track record and whether the task is consistent with their roles and responsibilities. It can also be used as a technique for development. Here you can ask, 'Who could benefit from the experience of performing this task?'

Increasing use of empowerment in organizations is helping managers to delegate more. However, if an organization has empowerment built into its corporate philosophy or mission statement, it is important to explain to employees what they're empowered to do. Bureaucracy and red tape are major barriers to delegation, whereas empowerment is a major solution.

Note that steps 1 to 3 are 'set-up' activities that the manager must carry out before they actually delegate the task.

4 Describe the end result required to the direct report or team member. Describe exactly what is required, eg a verbal report, an e-mail, a memo, a written recommendation, a PowerPoint presentation, a visit to a client, etc. It is important to emphasize results, not methods.

5 Explain why and where. Explain why the task has to be done in the first place and where it fits in the overall scheme of things. In other words, explain the job context and emphasize the individual's contribution to the department or the organization in carrying out the task.

6 State the required completion time of the task, eg 'By 3 o'clock, Friday, 1 December.' Avoid such terms as 'as soon as possible', 'at your earliest possible convenience', 'when you finish what you're doing' or 'when you get a chance'. Such terminology is imprecise and can lead to crises.

7 Indicate the appropriate degree of effort to be applied, eg should the direct report or team member drop everything else and concentrate on the task, or should they fit it in with their normal work? This is about identifying priorities.

8 Obtain the individual's own input. Encourage them to make suggestions and/or recommendations, to ask questions, to discuss use of resources, etc. Remember that delegation is a form of development. Let them use their own discretion and initiative in carrying out the task.

9 Come to an agreement as a result of your discussion with the direct report or team member as to what resources they may require to carry out the task, ie be specific about their authority. Also make sure it is sufficient.

10 Verify understanding of the task. Ask open-ended questions (those that cannot be answered 'Yes' or 'No') to check understanding. Avoid having the individual simply repeat the task outline or the whole task word for word. It is important to be sensitive when asking someone if they understand something. Some people can become defensive. This can be overcome by taking on yourself the responsibility for the quality of communication. You could say something like 'I just want to make sure I explained this properly. Could you put it in your own words to verify we both have the same understanding?'

   Complicated tasks can be followed up with written confirmation of the details, to guide the direct report or team member and serve as a reference later on in evaluating performance of the task. If the previous steps have been covered effectively, then this should not present a problem.

11 Establish checkpoints for reviewing progress. In complicated tasks, establishing review dates will assist the manager in monitoring progress and provide an opportunity for the direct report or team member to ask further questions about the task if necessary. This is the control mechanism. If something is not on target, this is the time to correct it. This monitoring technique helps prevent subsequent crises.

12 Follow through by asking for the results when the deadline has arrived. If closure on the task has not been obtained, the individual may conclude that it was only 'make work' ie work for the sake of work. This can have a demotivating effect on them.

13 Provide feedback on the total activity (use of methods, resources, timing, etc) in discussing the results of a task. Avoid
concentrating on negatives. Ensure that the recognition of
results is appropriate to the effort. Positive reinforcement for
a job well done can have a powerful impact.

Following these steps when delegating will ensure that both the
manager and the direct report or team member know what is to
happen and when. In tasks of a recurring nature, not all steps
would necessarily be followed unless the manager was doubtful
of the individual's ability to carry them out, or did not know them
very well.

In receiving tasks from their own boss, the manager should
apply the steps in this process, as appropriate, by identifying any
missing elements and proposing how they might be covered.

What if the direct report or team member refuses?

A major factor in the success of any delegation arrangement
rests on the quality of the offer–acceptance process between the
manager and their staff or team members. This in turn depends
on the basis of trust that exists between them. The direct report or
team member may seek to avoid delegated activities if they:

■ fear adverse criticism if they make a mistake;
■ lack motivation and can see no obvious quid pro quo, present
or future;
■ feel that any incentives offered do not balance the risks or
consequences of failure;
■ lack confidence in their own ability, or are by nature defensive;
■ mistrust the manager's motives or readiness to stand by them
in adversity;
■ are accustomed to being told exactly what to do under per-
petual close supervision;
■ are left with a sink-or-swim impression;
■ are given not a whole task to manage but only part of one.

Where there is a negative response from staff, the responsibility rests with management to create an environment that encourages delegation, with its accompanying degree of risk, and that rewards positive responses. When delegating for the first time, it is often desirable for the two parties involved to write down their respective expectations and interpretations of what is required and to compare notes before the arrangement is finalized. A record should then be made of what has been agreed between them and each should retain a copy.

If a direct report or team member fails to make a success of the assignment delegated to them, ask yourself:

Is it confidence or ability that is lacking? Why is this so? Did I select the right person; if not, why not?

Has the direct report or team member been given an adequate opportunity to acquire and demonstrate the knowledge and skill required?

Have I been exercising the right amount and style of support/ supervision?

Has the direct report or team member been encouraged to see this as an opportunity for self-development and am I showing adequate interest in their progress?

Delegation is not abdication. It is necessary to follow up. This is the control mechanism of management. The word 'control' has taken on a negative connotation in this age of empowerment. However, it is necessary. For example, had there been proper controls in place at Enron and Nortel, their problems might never have occurred. To assist in this follow up, we recommend use of the chart in Figure 18.4. The chart is for use with direct reports; it is assumed that you have a file (electronic or otherwise) for each of your direct reports. A similar chart can be used with team members.

In today's world with more hot-desking, people working from home, flexi-time and the like, effective delegation assumes an even greater importance.

Name:..		Title:..		
Date	Task description	Review date	Due date	Comments

Figure 18.4 Delegation chart: direct report

19

Effective meetings

If we didn't have so many meetings, we might actually get some work done.

Disgruntled manager

Numerous studies have shown that managers spend at least 30 per cent of their time in meetings. Meetings are seen as a good way to stimulate discussion and an effective and democratic way to communicate with people. Some people believe meetings lead to better decisions. But unfortunately, many meetings are held not to make decisions but to avoid them. They diffuse responsibility so that if something goes wrong, fault is spread.

Meetings take one of two forms: regular meetings and those with a limited life. If the former, they can outlive their usefulness. Occasional surveys should be conducted on whether they are necessary. In practice, many no longer have a clear and useful purpose, and even if they have, they are often not effective in achieving it.

Within organizations a major problem can be with regular, ongoing, cross-departmental committees, particularly those with decision-making authority. Departmental managers see these as dangerous bodies that can limit their freedom, priorities and allocation of resources. Accordingly, there is a tendency for senior staff to attend for status reasons, and for the committees to become a focal point of power struggles. In reality, more junior and knowledgeable people should be there, although if this happens they are often given instructions on the 'party line' that they should follow. In consequence, decisions may not be in the best interests of the organization.

When trying to make decisions in groups, the presence of some members may intimidate others. The words of group presidents and chief executive officers are given higher credence and they tend to dominate group situations, with their ideas being frequently accepted without question by the yes-men or -women. The danger then is that if resistance is not open, it takes the form of withdrawing interest instead. Linked with this is what psychologists call 'evaluation apprehension', where those voicing unpopular, albeit correct, ideas may breed conflict, which can be a career-limiting move.

If you think you spend too much time in meetings, you should cost this time. Complete the exercise in Table 19.1 to estimate how much meetings are costing your department. If someone gets all the departments in the organization to do the same, you'll get a rough idea of how much meetings are costing your organization.

When you have completed Table 19.1, add your total in F to that of other members of your department and work out your departmental average.

Of course, other costs are incurred that do not appear in the table. The main one is the opportunity cost. In other words, people attending meetings are not seeing to other duties. If a group of sales people are in a meeting that does not include clients, they are not making sales. If the meeting is held off-site, the associated costs climb steeply, eg transport, meals, equipment, room-hire fees.

Because of the amount of time consumed daily in meetings and their accompanying costs, it is important to make sure that these meetings are productive. The good news is that there are techniques for achieving this.

Meeting purpose

Before holding a meeting, it is essential to know its purpose. This should be communicated to those attending. When people meet regularly, the purpose may begin to alter with time, and meetings can take on a life of their own.

Even when the purpose is clear and has been communicated to attendees, the meeting may still not be effective. It may be that the wrong people are attending; or when the right people attend, there may be a failure to develop a balance between a sense of solidarity and focus on the task in hand.

Table 19.1 Cost of meetings

1	Estimate the number of meetings you attended last month. Don't include meetings with clients or with your boss. Include only meetings which three or more people attended.	A: number of meetings
2	Estimate in hours (or part hours) the average duration of meetings attended.	B: average duration
3	Calculate the number of hours you spent in meetings last month.	C: multiply A by B
4	Calculate the number of hours spent by all people in the meetings you attended. Multiply C by the average number of people at each meeting.	D: hours spent by all people in meetings
5	Calculate monthly payroll cost of meetings you attended. Multiply D by the average hourly cost (salary plus benefits plus perks) of attendees. Make a calculated guess for the salaries, etc of other attendees.	E: monthly payroll cost of meetings attended
6	Calculate annual payroll cost of meetings attended. Multiply E by 12.	F: annual payroll cost of meetings attended

Planning a meeting

The exercise we suggest here will help you plan and organize meetings, with the following benefits:

- it provides you with the purpose of the meeting;
- it allows you to determine the best approach;
- it enables you to prioritize the agenda;
- it gives you the opportunity to make last-minute changes prior to the start of the meeting;
- it gives you a 'track' to run on and helps you to identify timing problems;
- it helps identify possible problems and/or conflict situations, and plan appropriate avoiding action;
- it gives you the opportunity to assess your degree of success after the meeting. The box below summarizes key points requiring particular attention.

Aspects of effective meetings

There are two aspects to making meetings work effectively:

1 Structure:
   - clear purpose;
   - right size;
   - effective planning;
   - effective preparation.
2 Interpersonal relations:
   - listening skills;
   - building on ideas;
   - effective chairing.

Effective chairing is essential. It may include gatekeeping, ie more aggressive participants must be controlled and everyone drawn in. It also includes the ability to clarify and summarize.

Preparation checklist

Managers live in a swirl of meetings, but even in good organizations many meetings are poorly run because no one has taught people how to manage them effectively. The following points may be helpful:

Agenda and meeting aids:
- Have you determined and documented in point form all the items you wish to cover?
- Have you allowed time for discussion?
- Have you obtained, prepared and familiarized yourself with charts, case studies, demonstration CDs, DVDs, etc, if they are to be used?
- Have you sufficient information relating to the items to be discussed? Adequate data are essential. A lack of them is one of the greatest causes of meeting failure. The facts may be readily available or they may require some real digging out beforehand. To assume that someone will turn up at the right moment with the right data can be disastrous.
- When vital facts are missing, the meeting may wander around and finally break up for lack of information. Or members may debate endlessly around the issue, dodging the lack of facts. Most hazardous of all, they may argue on a compromise of the facts and proceed to a decision on the basis of guesswork.

Table 19.2 may assist in the planning of the meeting sequence.
Meeting plan:
- Have you worked out a logical approach to the meeting?
- Have you analysed the group and tried to anticipate probable individual responses and group reactions?
- Have you sought to identify experiences that can be elicited from the group as a basis for discussion?
- Have you determined ways of getting full participation, of stimulating thinking and maintaining interest, eg

Table 19.2 Meeting agenda

Purpose of meeting:			
Start time:			
Finish time:			
Item	*Responsible*	*Time*	*Discussion Information Decision Action*

soliciting opinions, using open-ended questions, group
tasks?
- Have you anticipated the probable direction of the group's
conclusions and considered reasonable or possible
solutions?
- Will everyone's schedule allow time for proper coverage
of the subject?
- Should the meeting be held now or later; are the others
ready to meet now?

Notification:
- Has everyone been given adequate notice of the time and
place of the meeting, its subject, agenda, support docu-
mentation and any suggested preparatory reading or
thinking?
- Who should attend the meeting?

Attendees:

The problem in running effective meetings grows exponentially with size. An optimum meeting size is usually five to eight. Too few attendees may result in a failure to spark off from each other, while more than eight may make it difficult to get everyone involved. One of the reasons why many meetings fail is having the wrong people present. Another common mistake is to have too many people, including deadweights – those who are not directly involved or are not close enough to the subject to contribute effectively. Also, meetings should not be used to deal with matters that are better handled by an individual.

A general rule about who should attend is not to bypass anyone who will be required to put the plan into operation. If you feel that a certain person will block the plan and you bypass them, then you've just made sure that that person will block it. Getting people involved in a problem is a good technique for solving it.

Finally, consider whether everyone needs to attend the entire meeting. Your aim is to have the minimum number of people present in order to get the best results. This could therefore be:

- someone who has all the facts;
- someone who will have to carry out the decision;
- the person in charge of the project;
- anyone whose department will be involved later on;
- a good ideas person;
- anyone whose moral support is needed on the project;
- anyone who might profit from the experience of attending.

Timing:

Meetings have a tendency to go on for far too long. So:

- Plan carefully so that adequate time has been allotted for each phase of your discussion.
- Anticipate not meeting your objectives within the allocated time. If you feel there is too much to handle in the time you have allotted, it may be better to schedule another meeting at a later date than to try to rush items through or run over the time scheduled.

One hour is long enough for most meetings. However, the length will vary depending upon the material you want to cover. A meeting worth having should not run less than 30 minutes. Only in extreme cases should a meeting run more than two hours.

- Be punctual with your meetings. Initially, problems may arise because of cultural difficulties. It may be necessary to learn to manage this. Similarly, if the meeting is to finish at 11.00 am, be sure it finishes at that time. You won't get much attention from the members during the time it runs over. They may be physically present but psychologically absent.

Physical arrangements:

- Are air-conditioning, ventilation, humidity, light, heat and other controls properly adjusted?
- Have you made certain that suitable support equipment is available: chairs, tables, whiteboard, special props, pens, notepaper, flip charts, projectors, screens, microphones, etc?
- Is the seating arrangement the best that can be devised for the number of participants?

   People attach importance to how furniture is arranged. If you arrange it in rows facing the front, it looks like a schoolroom with the chairperson as schoolteacher. The likely result is that people won't talk much or ask questions. Also, it is difficult for people to hear others in this arrangement.

   It is better to arrange people in a circle, a U shape or around a conference table. This suggests that everyone present is equal, and the participants will feel more like talking. This arrangement also makes it easier for people to hear each other and read facial expressions – factors that are all part of the communication process.

   When a problem is under discussion, it may be appropriate to go to the site of the problem. The issue can then be discussed with employees on the spot instead of hearing about it second hand.

Opening remarks:
- Have you determined your opening remarks? These should be appropriate to the purpose, whether formal or informal, brief and to the point.
- Have you sufficiently clarified the reasons for the meeting and what it is supposed to accomplish? Keep your attendees informed.
- Is a problem to be resolved and, if so, have you made the group sufficiently aware of the *real* problem needing a solution?

Breakfast meetings

To accomplish more, a growing number of executives hold early-morning business meetings over breakfast. At lunch more serious discussion does not begin until the main course. Small talk dominates the drinks and appetizer period. But at breakfast meetings, because of the need to get to work, meetings are shorter, so small talk is avoided. Further, the cost is only a fraction of that of lunch or dinner. Overall, there is more of a sense of urgency to achieve the purpose of the meeting.

Closing the meeting:
- Does your outline include a framework for your closing remarks, reminding you to summarize and review the discussion and conclusions reached?
- Have you reminded yourself to stress the application or consequences of the meeting as they relate to the participants?
- Have you planned to end on a high note of enthusiasm?
- Have you specified who will do what and when?
- Smile and thank the attendees.

Improving meeting leadership

It is important that the manager understands how to improve their work with meetings. Some techniques are:

- Help the meeting decide clearly its purpose. It is important at the beginning of any meeting that it has a clear understanding of the goals it wants to reach.
- Help the meeting to become conscious of its own process. If a meeting is going to improve its operational efficiency, it must see the desirability of looking at its own procedures. Then the members will learn to take responsibility for how they operate and will realize that by improving their process they can improve their problem-solving ability.
- Help the meeting to become aware of talents, skills and other resources existing within its own membership. Some of the quiet members of the group will be potential sources of help on the matters being discussed.
- Develop group methods of evaluation so that the meeting can have ways of improving its process. This evaluation helps the chairperson and members to become aware of how the others feel and think.
- Help the meeting to learn to accept new ideas and new members without conflict, to learn to accept discipline in working towards long-range objectives and to learn to profit from failure. Often we can take advantage of a poor meeting by attempting to turn its frustration into new motivation instead of letting it become a symbol of defeat.
- Help the meeting to create new jobs or subgroups as needed and to learn to terminate them or the main meeting group itself, when the time is right.

The role of the chairperson

The chairperson has a key role to play in a meeting. Their principal tasks are:

- To stimulate interest in the subject.
- To keep the group intact and working as a team.
- To keep the meeting on track and away from issues that have nothing to do with the subject or are not on the agenda.

  When the meeting is a problem-solving one, people's hidden agendas, vested interests and the way they have been told to act often get in the way of a good discussion. The best way to get people back on the right track is to keep asking the following questions or variations of them:

  - What will be the effect of the proposal on the whole organization: this year, next year, five years from now?
  - Who will profit most from the proposal? How can we be sure the benefit will be a good one? Will it be at someone else's expense? If so, whose?
  - Who stands to lose because of the proposed course of action or interaction? How can the loss be minimized? Is the sacrifice really worth it? If so how can the losers be recompensed?
  - What will be the consequences as seen by top management, clients, the public?
  - Will we be proud of our action or inaction after the 'heat' is off us for a decision? Can we live with our consciences? Will we be willing to explain our decision to our families, our direct reports, our professional peers or other team members?
  - Are we trading a short-term plan for a long-term one? Are we compromising a higher value for the sake of one lower on our scale of values?

- To make sure that the members feel free to speak and express their opinions.
- To separate people's thoughts from their personalities. It may be harder to accept the good ideas of a person you dislike.
- To avoid monopolizing the meeting.
- To prevent any other individual from monopolizing the meeting.
- To make sure some desired action takes place as a result of the meeting.
- To focus on total agreement for an action or consensus, rather than getting a majority vote.

- To ensure there is a record of each meeting through the taking of minutes.
- To start and end on time.

Time

Following the meeting, the chairperson should ask if the objectives were met in the allocated time. Were they met completely, not at all or partly?

If the objectives were not met, why not? What, if anything, should the chairperson have done differently relating to:

- objectives;
- selection of participants;
- preparation of agenda and distribution;
- timing;
- location;
- layout;
- the chairperson's preparation;
- the meeting introduction;
- the chairperson's degree of participation;
- participation by meeting members;
- summing-up;
- follow-up?

Meeting minutes

The chairperson should not take minutes. If possible, one of the members should be selected for this job. The chairperson will be busy enough handling the discussion without having to take notes.

The following identifying information is suggested for meeting minutes:

- division, department, team, group;
- date;

- place;
- those present;
- those absent with apologies;
- those absent without notification;
- who conducted the meeting;
- distribution list of minutes;
- time meeting started and ended;
- signature of the person who took the minutes.

Minutes, however brief, should be kept of each meeting. They will provide a record of items discussed. They need not be elaborate. They should be brief, accurate and complete, covering:

- whether the minutes of the previous meeting were read and approved;
- all items discussed;
- agreements reached;
- action agreed upon, and who will do what and by when;
- items left open and their status;
- motions, plus mover's and seconder's names.

The minutes should be distributed as quickly as possible to all attendees and any other relevant persons.

In taking minutes, some key principles apply:

- Don't record every minor detail and every thought. The phrase 'after discussion' covers a lot of ground.
- Record the originators of suggestions if the suggestions are accepted.
- Avoid expressing personal opinions, interpretations or comments such as 'a great idea', 'a persuasive argument', 'a brilliant report', 'a super suggestion'.
- Take notes in enough detail and with enough accuracy to prepare complete minutes later on.
- Before writing minutes, there should be a brief discussion between the minute writer and the chairperson about context, to avoid errors and omissions.

■ The minutes should contain the day, date, time and place of the next meeting.

Post-meeting observations and evaluations

When the meeting is over and the last person has left, you as chair-person should ask yourself, 'How did I do?' As a conscientious manager concerned with doing a good job, this is important to you.

You will ask such questions as: Did everyone leave feeling they got something out of the meeting? Did everyone participate fully?

This is what may be termed a post-mortem. It is an attempt to determine whether or not the session has met the established objectives. This can lead to a change of method or a change of content.

The evaluation will help you to analyse the effectiveness of the meeting and to determine how you should improve your knowledge and skills.

Evaluation of effective chairing

The purpose of this is to ask yourself:

■ What were the objectives of the meeting?
■ Were they all accomplished?
■ If not all of them were accomplished, which ones were?
■ And which were not; why not?

You can share Table 19.3 with meeting members and use the feedback you receive as an evaluation tool.

With this feedback and the other techniques provided in this chapter you are now in a position to conduct effective meetings. No more will the attendees at your meetings be in a position to say, 'That meeting was a waste of time.'

Now it is up to you to take control of your life and your time.

Table 19.3 Meeting evaluation form

Please indicate your views on these aspects of the meeting on a scale of
1 to 5.

	Low				*High*
	1	2	3	4	5

Agenda

To what degree was the agenda followed?

Meeting objectives

To what extent were the objectives reached?

Time

Did the meeting start on time?
Were the allotted time frames adhered to?
Did the meeting finish on time?
To what extent was time used well?

Participation

Was a friendly atmosphere established and
maintained?
To what degree did everyone participate?

References and further reading

Alessandra, T (1996) *The Platinum Rule*, Warner Books

Berne, E (1964) *Games People Play – the basic handbook of transactional analysis*, Ballantine Books, New York

Briggs Myers, I (1987) *Introduction to Type: A Description of the theory and applications of the Myers-Briggs Type Indicator*, Consulting Psychologists Press Inc, Palo Alto, CA

Drucker, P F (2006) *Classic Drucker: Essential Wisdom of Peter Drucker from the pages of Harvard Business Review*, Harvard Business Press, Harvard

Gabarro, J J and Kotter, J P (1993) *Managing Your Boss*, Harvard Business Review Classics, Harvard

Gittelson, B (1975) *Biorhythm, A Personal Science*, Arco Publishing Company Inc, New York

Jones, L (1999) The Johari Window, *Business Executive Journal*, **13** (75)

Mintzberg, H (1990) The Manager's Job: Folklore and Fact, *Harvard Business Review*, May/June

Nichols, R G and Stevens, L A (1957) *Are You Listening?*, McGraw-Hill, New York (for details of the research in General Electric and Pfizer referred to in Chapter 14)

Parker, D and J (1988) *The Future Now*, Mitchell Beazley International (for the work of Hans Schwing and Reinbold Bochon, and the studies in the Omega Watch Corporation, the Ohmi Railway Company, the civic transport system in Zurich and the US National Lead Company referred to in Chapter 7)

Peters T J and Waterman, R H (1982) *In Search of Excellence*, Harper & Row, New York

Seeley, M and Hargreaves, G (2003) *Managing in the Email Office*, Butterworth Heinemann, Oxford

Stewart, R (1991) *Managing Today and Tomorrow*, Palgrave Macmillan, Basingstoke

Wass, D L and Oncken W Jr (1990) Who's Got the Monkey?, *Harvard Business Review*, January

The authors have also drawn on the work of Charles Handy, details of whose publications may be found online at www.wikipedia.org

Index

NB page numbers in *italic* indicate figures or tables